W9-AJR-708

How to Be
Hap-Hap-Happy
Like Me

ALSO BY MERRILL MARKOE

What the Dogs Have Taught Me
Late Night with David Letterman: The Book (*Editor*)

HOW TO BE HAP-HAP-HAPPY LIKE ME

MERRILL MARKOE

VIKING

VIKING
Published by the Penguin Group
Penguin Books USA Inc., 375 Hudson Street,
New York, New York 10014, U.S.A.
Penguin Books Ltd, 27 Wrights Lane,
London W8 5TZ, England
Penguin Books Australia Ltd, Ringwood,
Victoria, Australia
Penguin Books Canada Ltd, 10 Alcorn Avenue,
Toronto, Ontario, Canada M4V 3B2
Penguin Books (N.Z.) Ltd, 182–190 Wairau Road,
Auckland 10, New Zealand

Penguin Books Ltd, Registered Offices:
Harmondsworth, Middlesex, England

First published in 1994 by Viking Penguin,
a division of Penguin Books USA Inc.

1   3   5   7   9   10   8   6   4   2

Copyright © Merrill Markoe, 1994
All rights reserved

The following selections were previously published,
some in different form: "Let's Party," "When You
Wish Upon a Star Person," "Blind Date with the
Universe," "After the Beep," "House and Karma,"
"Puzzled People Cannot Laugh," "New Things to Worry
About," "Merrill Markoe's Guide to Hollywood Boulevard,"
and "The Week of Not Just Feeling Great but *Being*
Great" in *L.A. Style*; "Dominatrix 101" in *Vanity
Fair*; "Life 102" in *New Woman*; "Deranged Love
Mutants: The Story of Romeo and Juliet" in the *Los
Angeles Times*; "What I Did on My Summer Vacation,"
"Rites of Purification, or How I Finally Threw Away
the Recipe for 'John Davidson's Turtle Brownies,' "
and "Secrets of the Love Trade" in *New York Woman*;
"Manners for the Millennium" in *Time*; "Stupid Old
Girl Scouts Again" in *The New York Times*; and "My
Romantic Dinner with Fabio" in *TV Guide*.

LIBRARY OF CONGRESS CATALOGING IN PUBLICATION DATA
Markoe, Merrill.
How to be hap-hap-happy like me / Merrill Markoe.
p.   cm.
ISBN 0-670-85332-1
1. Happiness—Humor.   I. Title.
PS3563.A6652H69   1994
814'.54—dc20   94–10344

Printed in the United States of America
Set in Garamond Light
Designed by Jessica Shatan
Illustrations by William Neeper

Without limiting the rights under copyright
reserved above, no part of this publication
may be reproduced, stored in or introduced into
a retrieval system, or transmitted, in any form
or by any means (electronic, mechanical, photo-
copying, recording or otherwise), without the prior
written permission of both the copyright
owner and the above publisher of this book.

To the memory of
four unappetizing young people
on a rock

ACKNOWLEDGMENTS

Thanks to Dawn Drzal, Polly Draper, Michael Wolff, Carol Gary, Robin McCarthy, Cynthia Heimel, Lewis, Tex, Bo, and Winky, my brother Glenn, Giulia Melucci, Melanie Jackson, the United States of America, Fabio, and Warren Zevon

CONTENTS

How to Be Hap-Hap-Happy Like Me • 1

Happiness Hint #1: *Plan a party and invite the people you care about.*

Let's Party • 5

Happiness Hint #2: *Incorporate physical exercise into your daily routine.*

Zen and the Art of Multiple Dog Walking • 11

Happiness Hint #3: *Enroll in a class or lecture that interests you.*

Dominatrix 101 • 17

Happiness Hint #4: *Take the time to improve your knowledge of another period of history.*

Come Dine with Me in 1093 • 25

Contents

Happiness Hint #5: *Do something nice for an animal.*

PETS AND THE SINGLE GIRL • 31

Happiness Hint #6: *Sit down and really talk to someone visiting from another country.*

WHEN YOU WISH UPON A STAR PERSON • 37

Happiness Hint #7: *Curl up in bed with one of your favorite books.*

AMY FISHER: *MY* STORY • 45

Happiness Hint #8: *Attend a trade show or convention.*

ONE OF THE MOST THRILLING DAYS OF MY LIFE • 53

Happiness Hint #9: *Develop your own philosophy of life.*

LIFE 102 • 59

Happiness Hint #10: *Pamper yourself with a day of beauty.*

MY YEAR OF HEALTH AND BEAUTY FOR *YOU!* • 65

Happiness Hint #11: *Push your sense of romance to the next level.*

BLIND DATE WITH THE UNIVERSE • 71

Happiness Hint #12: *Do something you've always secretly wanted to do.*

A TOUR OF THE MOVIE STARS' HOMES • 77

Happiness Hint #13: *Conduct a meeting with all the members of your household.*

GREETING DISORDER • 83

Happiness Hint #14: *For at least a weekend, don't answer your phone.*

AFTER THE BEEP • 87

Happiness Hint #15: *Think up a creative way to celebrate a special occasion.*

DERANGED LOVE MUTANTS: THE STORY OF ROMEO AND JULIET • 93

Happiness Hint #16: *Devote a day to a real, old-fashioned spring cleaning.*

ANATOMY OF A MESS • 97

Happiness Hint #17: *Spend time visiting your own hometown as though you were a tourist.*

MERRILL MARKOE'S GUIDE TO HOLLYWOOD BOULEVARD • 103

Happiness Hint #18: *Start to write your own book or short story.*

WOMEN WHO HONK WITH THE GEESE • 109

Happiness Hint #19: *Redecorate your home to really please yourself.*

HOUSE AND KARMA • 115

Happiness Hint #20: *Visualize a future in which the world will be a better place.*

Manners for the Millennium • 121

Happiness Hint #21: *Attend a local production of a play or musical.*

Puzzled People Cannot Laugh • 125

Happiness Hint #22: *Do something completely out of character for you.*

How to Please a Man Every Time and Have Him Okay Maybe Not Beg for More but at Least Not Demand a Whole Lot Less • 129

Happiness Hint #23: *Treat yourself to something you never thought you could afford.*

A Tenacious Grasp of the Obvious • 135

Happiness Hint #24: *Throw out things that are no longer a part of your life.*

Rites of Purification, or How I Finally Threw Away the Recipe for "John Davidson's Turtle Brownies" • 143

Happiness Hint #25: *Come up with an idea for a new business.*

Stupid Old Girl Scouts Again • 149

Contents

Happiness Hint #26: *Take the time to look for signs of hope.*

IT'S A WONDERFUL LEWIS • 155

Happiness Hint #27: *Increase your knowledge of something that intrigues you by reading at least two books on the subject.*

SEX—WHAT, IF ANYTHING, HAVE WE LEARNED? • 159

Happiness Hint #28: *Risk meeting people in brand-new ways.*

THE SOULMATE DIARIES • 165

Happiness Hint #29: *Read a section of a newspaper or magazine that you ordinarily skip.*

NEW THINGS TO WORRY ABOUT • 173

Happiness Hint #30: *Brainstorm with a friend about alternative careers.*

SECRETS OF THE LOVE TRADE • 179

Happiness Hint #31: *Go out and attend a state fair or a circus.*

WHAT I DID ON MY SUMMER VACATION • 187

Happiness Hint #32: *Order a gift for yourself from a catalog.*

THE WEEK OF NOT JUST FEELING GREAT BUT *BEING GREAT* • 193

Happiness Hint #33: *Extend a social invitation to someone you've always been afraid to approach.*

MY ROMANTIC DINNER WITH FABIO • 199

How to Be
Hap-Hap-Happy
Like Me

How to Be
Hap-Hap-Happy Like Me

The reason I've called you all here today is to explain to you how you can be really happy. And I intend to do this despite the fact that I have no particular expertise in the field of mental health—a fact I want to make known right at the beginning before we are all dragged into the exhausting quagmire of emotional trauma that is bound to result from an exposé of my background. Besides, I guess it will come out eventually that there is little evidence that I myself have ever been particularly happy.

Yet why should I allow my apparent lack of qualifications to keep *me* from giving *you* advice? No one else does. In fact, I'm not sure that knowing nothing isn't an important prerequisite nowadays.

I think everyone will agree that happiness is a relative concept. "I'm not happy unless I have inmates brightening my day," Sue Harris, the woman in charge of the prisoner grievance committee at The Prairie Correctional Facility in Appleton, Minnesota, said to me. "When they fuck with my head it makes me happy." And while I admit that this particular scenario never seemed like a key ingredient in a happy life to *me,* it has also occurred to me that *my* version of a happy life was Frank Capra's vision of a tragic hell. When he wrote *It's a Wonderful Life* and was inventing the worst possible fate for the Donna Reed character in the event that the Jimmy Stewart character had never been born, he showed her looking well-groomed and fit, in a smart little two-piece suit, headed home after a long day of work. The first time I saw this, I thought to myself, "Hmm. Interesting. Apparently Mary did okay all by herself." That was before I realized that Frank Capra was forcing her to wear a slightly dorky-looking hat in order to warn us that he felt something was terribly wrong with this picture. And seconds later, a horror music sting accompanying the narrative clearly indicates how Frank Capra regarded the destiny he assigned her.

"What became of Mary?" Jimmy Stewart asks the angel.

"She never married," replies the angel, his voice quaking with emotion as though he were about to reveal that she'd been beaten to death with a rake. "There she is now. *She's closing up the library!!*" Frank Capra's vision of a woman with no reason to live: all dressed up in a suit, on her way home to an empty house, and, worst of all, condemned to make very bad hat choices. Wow. Talk about a waking nightmare. Here I thought my life was okay and whoops, silly me . . . turns out I'm actually a resident of hell.

With this as an indication that perhaps my instincts were not a good guide, I decided to try to pursue some more reliable, time-honored routes to happiness. Naturally the first important step I took was to purchase a "365 Days to a Happier Life" Desk Calendar. As I eagerly placed my mental well-being in the capable hands of a well-known greeting-card company, I vowed to follow all of their suggestions. I could feel my happiness level rise immediately.

Day one started out great. "Imagine your life has *just begun!*" was the first suggestion. Amazing. It worked. I was happier right away. "This is sensational," I thought to myself, "I am *one day old* and already a homeowner!!! Plus I'm *starting out* with the verbal skills of an adult. Maybe *now* I will have a shot at success on my own terms because I cannot fail to be instantly acknowledged as *the most incredible baby who has ever lived!* All I will have to do is show up *anywhere* in a diaper and read a few passages from *anything* and I will get *tremendous* response. At last, I have it made!!! The only thing that concerns me a little is the rate at which I'm aging. I mean, if I'm *starting out* looking like this, what can I expect by the time I hit high school? Won't I be much too old to hang out with 'the kids' in any kind of meaningful 'in crowd' position? I'll never get to be a cheerleader. I'll never get any dates. I'll be shunted aside, an eccentric loner forced to assume the role of the wounded, brooding artiste. Oh great. Even with *all these advantages* it's going to turn out just exactly the way it did last time."

Defeated and on the verge of a searing depression, I decided to skip day one and move ahead to day two. "Imagine you only have six months to live." Boy, there's a quick route to happiness. Immediately I went into a tailspin. "Oh God," I thought, "here I felt so well when I got up. And now I get this kind of news out of the blue. Can't I at least get a second opinion from another desk calendar? Man oh man, how am I supposed to keep getting happier and happier with a thing like this hanging over my head? I'd better drop everything and move to Rochester, Minnesota, to be near the Mayo Clinic."

Talk about a path to happiness gone completely awry.

Which brings me to *my* advice for *you*. It's very simple. Burn all your *other* happiness materials: desk calendars, day planners, short and long books, pamphlets, audio and video cassettes, essays, poems, and magazine article reprints. Even the ones by Marianne Williamson. Especially the ones by Marianne Williamson.

Now read *this* book. Because what *I* have done for you is to isolate and then carry out the very best of *everyone else's* "how to be happy" suggestions. By reading *my* book, you can become happier without ever having to leave the comfort and security of your very own private hell. Your only obligation will be the enormous debt of gratitude you will feel toward me for doing all the hard work for you.

And from now on, if anyone asks you what true happiness is, you can share with them what I have learned. Every moment of your life that is not a hideous nightmare *is* happiness. By that definition, you're happier than you thought! That, plus the thing about inmates fucking with your head. Turns out that was a very good suggestion!

HAPPINESS HINT # 1

Plan a party and invite the
people you care about.

• • •

LET'S PARTY

About once a year it occurs to me that I owe a lot of people a
social debt and really ought to have some kind of a party to try
and pay them back. I'm not saying I *act* on this impulse. I'm
just saying it occurs to me. And when it does, it is followed immediately by a sense of panic that makes me feel like one of
the members of that Chilean soccer team that survived an air
crash and had to contemplate eating a former teammate. In
other words, I freak. The next thing I do is begin paging compulsively through books on the subject of "entertaining at
home."

Of all the volumes in print on this topic, none fill me to
overflowing with as much simultaneous loathing and secret
envy as the combined oeuvre of Martha Stewart. Each one of
these intimidating tomes is expensively bound and bursting

with many, many beautiful color photographs featuring captions such as "a dramatic croquembouche surrounded by fresh flowers makes a spectacular centerpiece on the table in the library" or "Hepplewhite chairs, grandmother's plates, old silver, and long-stemmed Italian poppies grace the dining table set on our porch."

The author is a pretty blond woman with good bone structure and an uncanny ability to make whoever is her closest competitor for the title of Little Miss Perfect appear to have a learning disability. Her chapters have titles such as "Cocktails for 50—a festive occasion!" or "Summer Omelette Brunch Outdoors for 60!" I didn't even scan that one, since it is nearly impossible for me to get even one omelette out of a pan not looking like something I found at the bottom of my purse. But these are not the kinds of problems that plague Martha Stewart. "I always have baskets everywhere filled with fresh eggs," she tells us, perhaps while relaxing on the veranda of one of her summer homes in the mountain region of Neptune where I believe she spends a good deal of her time. Why? Because she simply gathers "eggs of all shapes, sizes, and hues from our Turkey Hill hens." She *has* her own hens. She has her own bees. She probably has a trout stream and a cranberry bog. She's always somewhere picturesque ladling something steaming into something gleaming.

The most pernicious thing about her is the way she makes the thing she recommends appear somehow vaguely doable. "To entertain at home is both a relief and a rediscovery," she says offhandedly, perhaps while seated pertly in the spacious living room of her weekend place on one of the moons of Jupiter. "It provides a good excuse to put things in order. Polish your silver. Wash forgotten dishes. Wax floors. Paint a flaking window sill." Of course it does. Especially during those long Jupiterian winters that I understand can go on for decades. *Nothing* puts *me* less in the mood for thankless chores than the swelling sense of panic that comes from planning a party.

So here at last is advice for people such as myself, busy, frazzled, with no innate hosting abilities or graces.

MERRILL MARKOE'S HOME ENTERTAINING GUIDE FOR THE PANICKY SOCIAL DEBTOR

CHAPTER ONE: PLANNING THE EVENT

1. The Guest List.

Martha Stewart says, "When you meet someone interesting at a party it is a natural reaction to think of all the other people who would like to meet him too. Sometimes I do this years in advance—putting people together in my mind." And I say to her, "Have a licensed professional sit you down and tell you all about lithium." *I* begin by inviting only those people I am so sure like me that virtually nothing I could say or do would sway their opinion. If this total does not get you beyond the fingers of one hand, add a select number of others who you know suffer from weight problems and/or eating disorders. These are people from whom heavy calorie consumption is always a problem so if you screw up the food, it won't matter. If it does happen, your guests will be secretly relieved.

2. The Menu.

Checking back in with Martha Stewart we learn that "a dramatic spicy taste is an inappropriate way to begin dinner." Therefore, it only makes good sense to begin by offering each and every arriving guest an enormous peppery bean burrito. "Cocktails that last much longer than an hour jeopardize the shape and momentum of the evening," Martha cautions. Since these are the very things that are most terrifying, figure on a two-hour cocktail period minimum. Now you've got everyone right where you want them: feeling fat and sleepy with a limited desire or ability to eat anything.

3. The Theme.

Martha Stewart says, "Your own dishes, possessions, and personality will determine the style and tone of the occasion." That is why I like to use as my theme "the breakup of the Soviet Union," my table settings and decorations reflecting with amazing accuracy the chaos, poverty, and desperation of a culture in the throes of disintegration.

Chapter Two: Day of the Party Preparations

1. As soon as you awake, begin your futile attempt to remove the vast quantities of pet hair that have settled over everything in your house like a gentle dusting of snow on a wintry morning. Pick up as many of the saliva-coated pet toys as you can find and hide them somewhere. Anywhere. Especially the squeaking vinyl turkey leg with a face.

2. Martha Stewart thoughtfully reminds us to "Remember to empty a coat closet" to accommodate the outerwear of your guests.

So, take all the stuff you have in there and move it to the . . . no, the garage is full. So is the bedroom closet. And the hall closet. Which is why I recommend that you just put everything *back* into the coat closet and lower the heat in the house so that your guests will not be inclined to take off their coats or sweaters.

3. Begin to anesthetize yourself. It may be politically incorrect in this day and age, but as much as you might like to, you *aren't* going to be driving anywhere. So isn't it worth it just this once to provide yourself with an impenetrable smoke-screen between your problems and anxieties and your own ability to perceive them?

4. Don't forget that "music can establish and sustain an easy mood." I prefer a simple loop tape of AC/DC singing "Highway to Hell." But select your own favorites, depending on your theme.

5. Clean the pet hair off everything *again,* making sure to notice that there is just as much this time as there was before you spent all those previous hours removing it. But this time, if you are sufficiently sedated, you may enjoy taking all the saliva-coated pet toys and assembling them into a colorful centerpiece, surrounded by fresh flowers and grandmother's old silver. Place the squeaking vinyl turkey leg with a face proudly in the front. Or go directly to

Plan B.
Turn out all the lights in your house and greet arriving guests in your bathrobe and pajamas. Wearing an expression of sym-

pathetic, quizzical bemusement, say to them, "Geez—this is kind of embarrassing. The party was *last* night. But hey— come on in. Can I get you a cup of tea?" They will probably stay only a few minutes—just long enough to get angry about already getting pet hair all over some cherished item of cloth- ing. But because the error will seem to be *theirs,* your social obligations will be paid in full!!

HAPPINESS HINT # 2

Incorporate physical exercise
into your daily routine.

• • •

ZEN AND THE ART OF
MULTIPLE DOG WALKING

I have four dogs. People say to me, "Four dogs! Why would you have four dogs? Isn't that too many dogs?" and I can only respond, "Yes. It's too many. I don't know why I have four dogs. Now please, please, just leave me alone."

Because I am not the kind of person who would *ever* give a dog away after I have fallen in love with it, I have learned to take a transcendent approach to the challenges presented to me by daily multiple dog management. After all, isn't that the true road to happiness? The ability to meet difficulties and obstacles with grace, energy, and good nature? Which is why I am able to offer:

Zen and the Art of Multiple Dog Walking

It is "walk time." You have put it off as long as possible. But the cyclone of dog activity whirling in the vicinity of the front door indicates that if you put it off much longer you could be eaten alive. So prepare yourself for the walk by focusing on the incredible joy you are bringing to these simple loving creatures who after all have not nearly as many creative outlets as you do.

As you get the leashes out, repeat this mantra: "I am one with the great joyous spirit that is all men and all beasts." Continue to say this as the dogs hurl themselves at you, knocking you over, making it almost impossible even to hook the leashes to their collars, let alone open the door. Somehow you must let out only two of them, which is the most you have determined you can ever walk safely at one time. Four of them at once is like waterskiing behind the space shuttle.

Having managed this, somehow proceed through the front yard with two fully leashed dogs under control while ignoring the pained, mournful yowls of the two dogs who remain behind, locked in the house. Tell yourself that the neighbors are *not* speculating about what mistreatment you are inflicting on these poor unhappy creatures. They probably can't even hear the ear-piercing shrieks. Certainly they *cannot* be as loud as you imagine.

Jauntily start out down the street, ready now not just to enjoy your "walk" but to appreciate the special way that two entirely different species of warm-blooded mammals can share a single leisure-time pursuit. Hold this thought for as long as possible, particularly when seconds later one of the two dogs wraps himself around a telephone pole and becomes impossible to unwrap because the other dog has continued moving forward in the original trajectory with the same velocity. Do not panic. You will not be ripped in half. Think for a moment about the complex geometry of nature. The way that the earth moves at one orbital speed and the moon and sun at others, while meteors and comets whiz by all over the place and yet there are no collisions. (Well, I suppose there are probably plenty of collisions. But none of them big enough to make the nightly news.)

No, instead they all harmoniously combine to make a perfect solar system, and so it will be with you and the dogs. In just a moment. As soon as you get the one dog untangled. So you call with increasing urgency for the other dog to "STAY!" as you begin to move in the direction in which the leash has wrapped itself around the pole, noticing with amazement how the dog proceeds ahead of you, maintaining a degree of entanglement exactly proportionate to your attempts to un-ravel him.

Do not grow irritable. Rather, think of the perfection in this movement. Not unlike the perfection of the way water swirls down a drain in one direction on one side of the equator and in another on the other side of the equator. Because so too does the other dog, who weighs 120 pounds, maintain a steady pull in the opposite direction—a pull that seems to be growing ever stronger because he is growling and arching. He is poised momentarily to begin a violent dog fight. The object of his hatred? A completely uninterested dog on the other side of the street who is roaming freely, unencumbered by human supervision. And as this dog gets closer, your dog begins bucking and snarling, baiting him. Calling him horrible dog epithets. Causing the hair on the neck of the other dog to suddenly stand straight up. Now it becomes apparent that he is in fact a street punk who has probably never lost a fight in his entire life. So you scream at your big fat lardass dog who eats health food and sleeps on your bed to "STAY! I SAID STAY! DON'T YOU MOVE ONE INCH OR I'M GOING TO FIGHT WITH YOU MYSELF!"

And somehow, through the infinite grace of the workings of the universe, for once in your pitiful life he pauses long enough for you to at least unwrap the other leash from around the damn pole. Just in the nick of time, too, because at this point the dog fight was so close to start time that the neighborhood children have erected bleachers and are selling refreshments. And *somehow* through a combination of menacing faces and jerky movements you also inspire the strange dog to head off on his own down the street.

Okay take a deep breath. Everything is fine. Harmony is once again restored. And now, it's finally time to "go for a walk" on this balmy summer day. Except this time a squirrel scampers by somewhere behind you, although you're not quite sure where. Both dogs pick a different angle of approach in their high-speed attempts to apprehend and kill him. Now suddenly you are wrapped in two leashes, each tightly wound around a different leg so that you look like some kind of overdressed, poorly planned bondage pictorial. And in the heat of the moment you are knocked to your knees and pulled forward toward a blind turn where none of the motorists speeding by will even be able to focus on you before they feel you beneath their tires. You know you have to get out of there fast, but you can't move either of your legs. And now your knees are scraped for the first time since you were seven.

"ASSHOLES! I SAID STAY!" you yell at your dogs, praying they accidentally decide to listen. It's happened before. If only it would happen again now. And magically, at the very last moment before you are meaninglessly mowed down by a well-meaning driver—a sacrifice at the shrine of dog recreation—*bingo!* They do! They actually STAY!!! Long enough for you to loosen the leather bindings from around your legs and get yourself back on your feet. And as you do, remind yourself of the incredible elegance of Newtonian physics. For every action there is an equal and opposite reaction. Yes! Everything synched up in a big cosmic tango.

But now your knees are bleeding and stinging so you gather the leashes tightly and march those two ungrateful animals back to the house, trying to remember to marvel at the uncomprehending, resilient expressions of joy they wear on their faces in spite of everything that has happened. You were almost killed. But as far as they are concerned, everything went very well.

Back in your home, you want to sit down in peace and quiet and bandage your knees—at least take a moment to recover from the trauma of a near-death experience. But of course the first thing you run into are the faces of the other two dogs who have done nothing since they saw you last but mourn your departure. Every molecule of their beings is alive with eager anticipation of the incredible good time they know you are going to show them. Oh well. Now you have no choice but to hook each of them up to a leash and repeat the entire process again with an all-new cast.

And this time, try to do it with more serenity, damn it.

Enroll in a class or lecture
that interests you.

• • •

DOMINATRIX 101

The class description in the course catalog that I picked off the
top of a pile on the floor of the frozen yogurt place asks a
question that speaks to my very soul: "Do you want to learn
how to make big money in a safe legal profession that will
never leave you bored?" The answer is Yes! Yes! A thousand
times yes!

That is just one of the reasons why I am among the fifty or
sixty women of every race, body type, and demographic sam-
ple profile who are filing into the conference room on the top
floor of that hallowed institution of higher learning—the Hyatt
Hotel on Sunset Strip in the heart of Hollywood. On our way
to our seats we all smile and say hello to a guy in a Hawaiian
shirt. In short order our teacher, a blond woman of about fifty,
appears at the front of the room. Dressed in a two-piece tur-

quoise suit with a bright yellow blouse and sporting a short sensible haircut, she is almost unrecognizable from the shiny, leathery photo that she uses to advertise her class in The Learning Annex brochure. She is "Internationally Known Dominatrix Ava Taurel" and she is here to explain to us how to "Become a Dominatrix for Fun, Love and Profit." "Whether you want to enhance your relationships or become a professional dominatrix, this class will show you how." I find myself scrutinizing the perfectly random group of women around me, trying to guess who is here for which motive. It is impossible to tell.

"As you know, the class is for women only," Ava begins. "This upsets a lot of men. They have threatened to sue me for sex discrimination because they all want to come to the class. Right now they are hanging around down in the lobby, panting. But before we begin, I promised this one fellow he could speak with you for just a minute." The guy in the Hawaiian shirt steps forward. He tells us that he is a fitness trainer and a masseur and he just wants us to know that he is "available for whatever comes to mind so you can practice to be better dominatrixes." With that he distributes business cards to any interested takers and bids us a hearty farewell.

Now class is in session for real. To warm us up, Ava has spliced together a tape montage of famous scenes in the history of movies involving female domination: Susan Sarandon tying up Tim Robbins in *Bull Durham;* Melanie Griffith tying up Jeff Daniels in *Something Wild;* Sharon Stone in just about anything.

I find myself succumbing to my old school behavior patterns: tugging at my hair, shifting in my seat, glancing at my watch. However, it is only when Ava begins a free-form Q-and-A session that I realize I'm not in Comp. Lit. anymore.

The first question comes from a cute blond girl in her early twenties wearing a baseball cap who explains that she has just gotten her first real job at a dungeon and wants to know whether or not she should buy her own equipment.

"It varies from place to place," Ava tells her, "but before you do, make sure they have good lockers." Good lockers. Write that down.

Next a hugely obese lady wants to know how to get started in her own business. Ava cautions her about working outside of a protected environment, then explains how it is a good idea to operate from an office that overlooks a pay phone so that you can scrutinize a potential client before you take him on. That would apply to *all* walks of life. Write that down too.

From there Ava is off and running on a topic she knows well—what it takes to be a *good* dominatrix. "A wicked imagination," she begins. Mmmhmm. I have that. "And you must be able to give a clear command with your eyes. Sometimes they are steel. Sometimes they are caring." Still sounds doable. "It's very important to improvise," she points out. Hey! I'm good at improv! For example, Ava once had a man dress up as a maid, wear jingle bells on his testicles, and walk up and down the halls of his apartment house ten times. I raise my hand. I want to know what the best adhesive is for attaching the bells. But the woman in front of me gets called on first. She says that she had the idea of making a man chew on a bone. "Very nice," says Ava, clearly impressed. "You must develop your own uniqueness."

My own uniqueness. Sounds promising.

Fondly Ava recalls the golden days when she had ten women with different uniquenesses working for her. "For instance, one woman might not like pain but might be very skilled at verbal abuse." Well, I'm certainly verbal. "Then again, I remember a man who was into eating his own shit. *I* couldn't work with him. *I* would start throwing up. But for a woman who could stand it, it was three hundred dollars for fifteen minutes." Time to stop taking notes. Another misbegotten career right down the drain.

Now it is intermission, and not a moment too soon. All around me, networking breaks out. Gals are mingling around a table, writing down the titles on the reading list (*The Correct Sadist: Step by Step How to Turn a Man into a Slave*), perusing the new issue of *Rubber and Rivets*. (The cover story boasts "Corsets aren't just for discipline anymore." Of course, I knew that.) "I'm a hypnotherapist and I teach a lot of mind games. You should give me a call," a distinguished-looking blonde in her early forties says to a plain pear-shaped woman in her early fifties.

When class resumes again, we meet another man. This one a fit attractive guy in his forties was *invited* by Ava. He drove over three hours from San Diego to volunteer his services. "He's a big strong man from the Navy Seals," says Ava, who orders him to take off his shirt and jacket before she will permit him to take questions from the group. An incredibly beautiful Asian woman raises her hand to ask a question. "Why don't you tell us about your background?" she requests. "Well, I'm from a small town in Pennsylvania," says the Seal. His dream was always to be a Navy Seal he tells us, "chasing bad guys all over the world." He has many tales of manly danger. He wants us to know he has worked with explosives and high-powered weapons. He wants us to know that he has jumped out of planes and dived deep beneath the sea. He wants us to know about all this macho stuff so we can understand why he needs the release from stress that only wearing women's underwear can give him. I am puzzled. Wearing women's underwear has never helped me with stress.

I glance across the aisle from where I am sitting. The attractive black woman in the gray suit seated beside me has closed her eyes and dozed off for a second. But she is jolted back to consciousness when Mr. Navy Seal agrees to honor a request from the group to show us the red garter belt and white ladies' nylons that he is wearing under his pants. What a picture he makes. It's too bad the Navy Seals don't have one for their brochure. "Yes, I like being restrained," he admits as he lets his pants drop around his ankles. "I'm into erotic pain but I don't like my arms to be dismantled or anything like that."

"Just a few more questions," says Ava, "because I want us to start using him for different things. I want the women to take turns and come up one after the other." She lays out an assortment of whips, ropes, leashes, collars, and other dog accessories on a table nearby.

It starts out slowly at first. The large pear-shaped woman in the pink sweater asks him to kiss her hands. He does. Then it starts to heat up. A pretty blonde in tight jeans commands him to straddle a chair butt outward so she can practice her whipping technique. She smacks him tentatively. "Those pants are pretty thick. You can hit him harder," Ava advises. "You want to aim at the broad part of the back, or the back of the legs. You want to avoid this area here because you can hurt the kidneys." I raise my hand. I want to know if this will be on the final exam. The blonde smacks him much harder on her next try. Then she leans over to see his reaction. "He's smiling," she reports back to the class. "Make him say thank you!" a class member yells out. "Do you want some more?" the blonde asks him. "Yes," he mumbles. "I can't hear you," she taunts him. The class applauds spontaneously.

The next woman up to bat is a plain, boxy Latino woman in her early forties, dressed in a black and white striped suit with a knee-length skirt. She commands the Navy Seal to get on his knees. "Kiss my feet," she orders. "That's it. I've been home all day and they do hurt. Take off my shoes and smell them. Oh? You think that's funny? Then put my leg between your thighs and hump it like the dog that you are." *And he does it.* Well, it *is* school. Maybe he's worried about his GPA. The class breaks out in applause again. I am thinking, *"Who are these people?"*

Whereupon a gorgeous white woman with long black hair and *enormous* breasts, dressed in a skin-tight red sweater and short black skirt, takes confident control of the Seal. She puts him into a dog collar, attaches it to a leash, and begins to lead him up and down the aisles. *Now* I'm angry. His leash technique is *sooo* much better than what I can get from *any* of my four dogs, even after all that expensive training. I can't take it anymore. I have to get out of here. This is the final insult!

"The lady who is leading him around the room is his wife," announces Ava. Happily reunited, the Seal and the babe take the stage and answer questions like they are a celebrity couple: The Liz and Larry Fortensky of Domination. "You never told me you like to be whipped," she teases. "He never liked to be whipped before."

"Really???" says the blonde who did the whipping, suddenly embarrassed and full of remorse. "I didn't know you didn't like to be whipped. Because I don't like to whip either. I guess I should have asked you first."

"Communication is very important," says Ava. "I guess we were both a little nervous," says the Seal. Everyone nods.

"Well, that's it for tonight," says Ava, "except for those of you who would like to work on knots." It's almost 11:00 P.M. I think I'll work on my knots in the morning.

On the way down in the elevator, a bunch of us compare notes. "It was either this or an antiques lecture. And the antiques lecture was sold out," says a very professorial looking black woman, waving goodbye as we head across the parking lot to our individual cars.

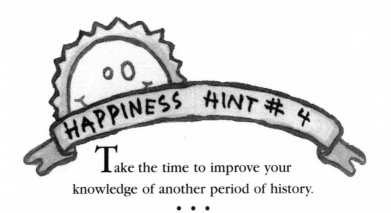

Take the time to improve your knowledge of another period of history.

• • •

COME DINE WITH ME IN 1093

They used to call it the Dark Ages when I was first learning the names of historical periods back in grade school. And that phrase still colors all my associations with the Middle Ages: feudalism, bloodletting and leeches, hooded monks chanting mournfully and flagellating themselves in dank, torch-lit corridors, chastity belts, the Hundred Years War, the Black Plague. And of course the more I dwell on these images, the hungrier I get for a three-course chicken dinner with herb-baked potato and a fruity wine cocktail. Which is why I am very lucky that one of the Medieval Times Dinner and Tournament Restaurant franchises ("where the year is 1093 A.D. and you are the guests of the royal castle") is only about a two-hour drive from my house. Talk about the promise of a rousing good time! Pinch me! I must be dreaming!

I probably would have gone there sooner, but until last week I could never get any of my so-called friends to say yes to an invitation to join me . . . even after I offered to pay! And it didn't really sound like the kind of place I could go to by myself and sit inconspicuously in a corner, pretending to be lost in important thought. So I was both impressed and grateful when my friends Polly and Michael not only didn't back out on me at the last minute but also didn't bolt out of the car as we turned into the parking lot of the only castle on the block.

"I didn't realize that the parking in the Middle Ages was this bad," Michael whines as he nervously comprehends for the first time what exactly he is going to be expected to put up with.

I myself begin to get swept up in the spirit of the Middle Ages (or maybe I just begin to feel middle-aged) pretty much from the moment I purchase our tickets next to the life-sized mural of the caped and armored knights of the realm, right beneath the giant sign welcoming all patrons to "Visit our museum of torture." Apparently back in 1093 that was what they did with their evenings instead of watching sitcoms.

Moments later Michael comes bounding back from the room labeled LORDS to report, "I hear a toilet flushing and a dude wearing a tunic and tights comes out and washes his hands."

"There was a woman in a long green gown with a veil and gloves in the next stall in the ladies' room," says Polly. So now we know for sure we're not in Kansas anymore. Although, who knows—Medieval Times is a chain. There *may* be one just like this in Kansas.

Anyway, first thing on the agenda is to partake of the medieval tradition of being photographed with an old bearded guy in a cape and a crown. No one seems to know who he is. We all keep our fingers crossed that he is not armed and does in fact have a job here. A quote in my orientation brochure reads "My noble guests, you honor me with your presence. I, Don Raimundo II, Count of Perelada, welcome you to my castle for an evening of sumptuous feasting and spectacular pageantry." I have a feeling this may be Don. And how interesting to note that in the ensuing eight hundred years the phrase "you honor me with your presence" has been changed to mean "You must pay me thirty dollars if you want to come in."

"Working here is just like being back in high school again," the "ticket wench" tells me after I finish having my picture taken. "The knights are the jocks. The managers are the principals. The tech crew are the druggies." I always suspected the Crusades were just a big pep rally. But before I even get to find out who the bartenders are, a couple of men in velveteen tunics carrying horns (the pep band?) step onto a little stage to call for our attention with a brief but alarming duet. "What do you call that kind of music?" I ask Michael, because he is a professional musician and I am an eager student of history. "I call that some sad shit," he replies.

Now a guy with a manicured beard wearing a robe and a cape comes forward to make some kind of proclamation. He is speaking with the kind of generic Shakespearean accent that could get him work selling mutton at a Renaissance Faire. His message elicits such wildly enthusiastic response from the crowd that I cannot hear what he has said. "Sorry, I didn't catch it either," the cheering guy beside me explains, not letting that dampen his enthusiasm. But no matter, because now it is time to take our seats at tables that surround a large exhibition ring. We are all wearing colored paper crowns that correspond both to the tablecloth colors and to the teams of knights for whom we are expected to cheer. Those of us who are attending unaccompanied by children under the age of ten are hoping we look like very good sports and not complete idiots.

"Hi. I'm Rick, your slave and manservant," says a guy in an apron and two different colors of pant legs. "M'lady, may I present your dinner?" Of course! Dinner presentation! Always a welcome part of the medieval dining-out experience. And so I have placed before me a small plate of middle-aged celery and a large silver cauldron of some kind of reddish canned soup. Simultaneously the air is filled with more staccato horn bursts ("Something from *Fiddler on the Roof,* I think," says Michael) and out into the ring rides a gorgeous young man upon a valiant steed. (Or maybe it was the other way around.) "The cute one with the really long hair is my boyfriend," whispers the "beverage wench" to me. I think she means the *guy.* "He works with L. A. Models. Care for another fruity wine cocktail this evening?" In the high school that is Medieval Times, she is a cheerleader. Manservant Rick is a shop teacher.

"Does the soup not please m'lady?" he nails me, paying what I am starting to feel is entirely *too much* attention to my eating habits. "No, no, it's fine," I lie, "I just have a little touch of the bubonic plague. But I think it's just the twenty-four-hour kind."

And now into the show ring a dark-hooded, hunchbacked monk appears in a cloud of smoke. There is a weird foreboding music and chanting that I can't quite make out. "Who *is* that?" I ask my manservant Rick. "I'm sorry," he replies, "I really can't tell you. I've only been working here about three weeks." "I used to know but I forgot," says the beverage wench. "I can go in the back and check for you. Anyone care for another fruity wine cocktail?"

"Let's move on to happier matters," says the emcee as the spooky monk suddenly takes a powder. "My lords and ladies! A toast! To the knights of the realm!" Everyone cheers as Don Raimunda drinks an entire goblet of something. I'm not sure why this gets cheers. Perhaps just to celebrate the fact that a guy his age gets paid to wear a crown and drink a beverage for a living. Pretty good gig!

"M'lady is not hungry tonight?" says manservant Rick, on my case again. "Are you not feasting well tonight?" He is starting to give me the willies. "Yes, yes, I'm feasting perfectly well to-night," I snap at him. Feeling guilty, I try to talk to him hon-estly. Turns out manservant Rick used to be a contractor who fell on hard times. "Ten ninety-three was a bad year for home improvement," says Michael.

Now all around us the cheering has grown intense as the knights on horseback in the arena knock themselves and each other out jousting and running relays. "The one in the red cape is also a professional surfer," the beverage wench tells me. "He just got engaged. Are you going to want to purchase any photos this evening?" Now she has the *nerve* to try to sell us mounted photos of a bunch of bleary-eyed jerks wearing paper crowns and drinking from goblets. Ha-ha-ha. They think they're so damned funny. Whoops! Those are pictures of us.

"We welcome here tonight fifty-eight strong from the King-dom of Shell Oil," booms our emcee. "Also, Jeffrey and Kimberly announce their engagement." I look over at my friend Michael. His crown is falling down across his nose as he slides into his "pastries of the castle." He has fallen asleep. It is now the unanimous opinion of the lords and ladies at our table that it's time to head back to the future, which looks a good deal more attractive than it did a few hours ago.

On the drive home we try to evaluate the lessons of history we have learned.

"It *was* just like the 1100s," says Michael. "The 1100 block of Broadway."

As for me, I am deeply relieved to be returning to a time when no one constantly monitors my food intake and calls me m'lady.

They say that those who do not learn from history are doomed to repeat it. So I would like to think that I learned as much as I was meant to because I really don't care to go through all of that again any time soon.

HAPPINESS HINT # 5

Do something nice
for an animal.

• • •

Pets and

the Single Girl

Being a single woman and living by yourself in the United
States of America in 1994 can be a very rough life. Okay . . .
it's a pretty loose definition of the word "rough." It's not
"rough" like living in Bosnia and dodging mortar fire. Or Rus-
sia in the midst of economic and cultural collapse. Or doing
anything at all in Somalia or the Sudan. Come to think of it, it's
not even "rough" like trying to be a single mother in *this*
country. Or being half of one of those ghastly couples who
are making a public descent into hell, like Burt and Loni or
Mia and Woody. Or even part of any less publicized troubled
couple, like the ones who call day and night on those radio
psychology shows or turn up on "Geraldo." I guess what I'm
actually saying here is that being a single woman and living by

yourself in the United States of America in 1994 is a pretty easy hand to play.

After all, you don't have to debate your every decision with a critical detractor; there's no one around to constantly remind you which of your habits make others insane. You don't have to cook if you don't want to. And then on the other hand, if you want to eat shamelessly and endlessly, there is no one to comment, "Geez, you sure pack it away." You can decorate eccentrically. You can hang around with worthless weasels and ne'er-do-wells. Overall, it's a relatively painless way of life. Sure, you have to attend to every exasperating detail of your day all by yourself. But come on—that's a small price to pay. In fact, maybe it's *too* small. Maybe things are just a little bit too easy.

When my dog Stan died, there were a couple of weeks when I lived pet-free. I fantasized that finally not being tied down to a dependent would give my spontaneous nature a chance to grow and flower. Then I realized that not only didn't I have much of a spontaneous nature but that the reason I wasn't partaking of the constant barrage of interesting activities and social events all around me was because I was a lazy sloth. Eventually this caused me to see myself in such an unflattering light that I had no choice but to go straight to the pound and come home with a puppy. And since that time, I have never had to look my own inadequacies squarely in the eye again because I have been blessed by the constant inconveniences of pet ownership. Which brings me to our topic here today:

THE IMPORTANCE OF PETS FOR SINGLE WOMEN

I. A bottomless source of guilt

A good, loving pet can provide his or her owner with reasons to feel guilty pretty much twenty-four hours a day—something that might be in short supply for the happy-go-lucky single woman. I have four dogs and every time I shift in my chair one of them gets up and runs to the door, wearing an expression on his face that reminds me of a small child on Christmas morning. If he could talk (and thank *God* he can't; I'm really not up to hearing him go on about butt itch) he would be saying: "Are you ready to go? You need a few seconds? Fine. I'll wait right here. Lalala two three four. How about *now?* No? Take your time. No problem. What about NOW? Okay. Fine. How about *NOW?*" And there I sit, knowing that while at no point did I have any intention of going anywhere, my cavalier lack of specific recreational intentions seems to have caused several creatures, whose only purpose in life is to show me constant love, intense disappointment if not searing depression.

And then, to make matters even worse, how about those occasions when I *do* have intentions to go somewhere but for wacky, selfish reasons of my own am planning to make the excursion unaccompanied by dogs? Now suddenly I am confronted with a sea of demoralized faces, silently blocking my path to the door, mouths agape as they beg me to reconsider the consequences of my actions. "You wouldn't enjoy yourself at my dentist," I explain to them. "The magazines are old. *No* dogs go to the dentist. Don't feel hurt. *No one wants* to get fitted for crowns," I say as I squeeze through the door with a heavy heart, wondering what kind of callow, unfeeling slob I am after all . . . only to return several hours later—tired and grumpy and sore—to be greeted by dogs who are *really* ready to go somewhere *now.* ANYWHERE. And this time they are *really not kidding.*

II. Dietary benefits

When you are single you tend to lapse into eating patterns that can be self-indulgent. But when you are a pet owner you never again have to worry about consuming a lot of empty calories because the motto of any self-respecting pet of any sort (in fact, a lot of them have it embroidered on pillows) is "Please. I'm starving. Let me have *all* of what you are eating right *now.*" To eat in the presence of most dogs is an experience not unlike sitting down to a picnic lunch in Bangladesh. And quite frankly, nothing puts a damper on the old appetite like many pairs of pleading, desperate eyes riveted to your every fork and mouth movement. This is something most pets are willing to do for you at all times, *regardless* of how recently they have been fed, thus enabling any reasonably sensitive person to lose three to five pounds a week with ease.

III. Practice for living with a significant other

Living with an actual man can have a variety of dangerous side effects. He can break your heart, threaten your sanity and your physical well-being, and cause you numerous personal and professional dysfunctions that can take years of costly and time-consuming therapy to unravel. So you don't want to mess with the wrong man: you have to choose your shots very carefully. On the other hand, you don't want to get so enamored of your own company that you get out of practice entirely and possibly lose the desire to cohabitate. (Or do you?

For the sake of argument, let's *say* you don't.) Pets can help to provide you with many of the same irritants that living with the man of your dreams will entail.

For instance, one of the hallmarks of every serious relationship I have had with a man has been uncomfortable sleeping circumstances. By this I refer to the cramped positions and rasping mouth noises that sleeping with a large unwieldy human male can often involve. And these inconveniences are cheerfully duplicated by any pet that you allow to share your bed (which in my case is every pet I have ever had). At first it is cozy and cuddly and cute—just like with a guy. And then, like with a guy, they fall asleep in some unlikely-looking position—adorable, trusting, and peaceful. And even as all the feeling in your legs begins to vanish, you are reluctant to wake them. When at last you do try to shift because you feel as though you may have severed your spinal cord, you realize that it is now impossible because they are dead weight—no easier to budge than a giant sack of lawn clippings. And so you wake the next morning, feeling as though you have been through hip replacement surgery, happy in the knowledge that your furry little pal hasn't missed any of his or her mandatory twenty-two-hours-a-day sleep.

IV. Practice for being a parent
Before a woman takes on the enormous responsibility of parenting, is it not a good idea to do a test run? This is where raising a pet can provide some interesting data. For instance, my dog Lewis, who is the only creature on the planet who truly reflects my influence (because he has lived with me since he was only six weeks old), is an overweight, whiny, badly groomed, poorly behaved, inconsiderate, and pointlessly de-

fiant giant boy who drools constantly and has incredibly high self-esteem. And so I have learned that any child of mine may well turn out to be an annoying big fat dumb guy who has no respect for the rights of others.

Lewis is currently dating one of my couches and seems to care nothing at all about the fact that he is also destroying the object of his affection in the process. This teaches me that I have also managed to duplicate in my dog the kind of behavior I have come to expect from the men I date. I don't know what the horrifying Freudian truth behind this fact might be, but I do know this: It would be in the best interests of everyone concerned for the government to pay me a monthly subsidy *not* to ever have children (much as they pay certain farmers not to grow crops). I think we all have quite enough to worry about as it is.

V. A flawless all-purpose excuse

When you are single you find yourself getting talked into attending a lot of functions you would avoid if you had any kind of *real* life. To say nothing of the potentially nightmarish circumstances provided by dating. In which case "I have to get home and let out my dog" will serve you much better and be kinder to say than "If I have to sit here and listen to one more tedious phrase tumble out of your big rubbery head I think I'm going to have to start taking hostages."

So—summing up—pet ownership offers the willing single woman a wonderful world of experiences and opportunities. At least that's what I keep telling myself when I wonder what in the world I've gotten myself into.

HAPPINESS HINT # 6

Sit down and really talk to
someone visiting from another country.

• • •

WHEN YOU WISH
UPON A STAR PERSON

The woman on the other end of the phone was looking for some advice about finding an agent. "We're debating who to contact," she explained to me, describing a scenario I've encountered dozens of times since I moved to Los Angeles. "We've channeled a film script that is really outrageously good," she went on, bringing front and center the detail that makes her version of this slightly different. Because of the thousands of people in the greater Los Angeles area who are looking for an agent, how many also have a 900 number on which to record the daily message they receive from "Lord Jesus Christ Sananda, Commander and Chief of the Intergalactic Confederation (Press one)" or "Mother Mary, Universal Director of the Feminine Christ Energy and Key Member of the Karmic Board (Press six)." Okay, maybe half a dozen . . . (this *is*

Los Angeles) but that's still a pretty small number for a city this size. And do the others also bring you the seven additional members of "the Spiritual Hierarchy and Ashtar command" such as "Commander Voltra" or "Zoser" or "Korton" or "Ashtar" himself? I think not.

The day I invested two dollars a minute for a three-to-five-minute message, Commander Jesus opened with "Greetings, Radiant One," then went on to offer advice such as "Make sure you want what you're thinking about. Karma can be instantaneous," immediately answering the question "How has His phrasing changed in the 2000 years since we spoke with Him last?"

As a person who was brought up without specific religious beliefs of any kind, I'm always fascinated by people whose worldviews provide them with all the answers. Aurora and Michael El Legion, directors of the Extra-Terrestrial Communications Network, are two people who seem to have very few unanswered questions. They live in a Malibu hillside condominium that they refer to in their printed material as "the launching pad." It may not be the only unit in the complex with a spectacular view of the coastline, but it is probably the only one that has a doormat that reads "Welcome UFOs and Crews."

Michael, an attractive, nattily dressed man of forty who came into this world as Mark Block, changed his name to El Legion "because it's a kind of a title. El stands for the Elder race. And Legion stands for the legions of volunteers." However, he's not talking about the same type of volunteers of which the Red Cross is so fond. He's referring to "star people," specifically, "those currently in an earth embodiment."

"I think it is important that the public is made aware of the

fact that we have *a choice* of the kind of extra-terrestrial beings we will have contact with," he tells me more than once in
the course of our discussion, which starts out at a million
miles an hour and never slows even slightly for the several
hours we spend together. "I've talked to 100 to 200 ex-military
intelligence people over the years and a lot of them tell me
that the whole agenda of certain people in the government is
to keep us unaware of the reality of UFOs. Their basic objec-
tive now is to tell everyone about 'the greys.' You've seen
them on TV. The ones with the big heads and the big eyes. Yet
they ignore any reference to the human-appearing extra-
terrestrials, the ones Aurora and I are in contact with, who are
very beautiful, benevolent beings."

"The greys," whom Michael believes have a pact with the
U.S. government that permits them to conduct abductions in
exchange for technology, "are considered renegades. They
are not even members of the Intergalactic Federation." I'm not
surprised. I never trusted them myself.

By this time, his wife of eleven years has joined us. Aurora
El Legion is a striking woman in her forties with straight black
hair. She is dressed in a black jumpsuit accessorized with long
silver earrings and a necklace bearing a crystal. Aurora and
Michael met at Arizona State University, where he was giving
a lecture on UFOs. Days before, when she was still Kathleen
Towne of Bloomfield Hills, Michigan, she had received a message during meditation that told her to sell everything and
move to Arizona, where she would meet her other half and
her true mission would begin. From the moment they spoke
at an intermission, they both *knew:* certainly my definition of
a good date. "I said to him, 'You know, I have just about all of
these star people characteristics. What do I do? Join a star peo-

ple country club?' " Aurora remembers fondly. "He started to
laugh and said, 'I want to see you after the lecture.' " And they
were together from that point on. These Star People work fast.
Then again, Michael never cared for dating. "I used to feel it
was a waste of time and energy," he explained to me, illumi-
nating the one thing *we* seem to have in common so far.

Of course, Aurora and Michael had some fairly unusual
things to bond over. Like early childhood experiences with
UFOs. "When I was eight, this guy actually walked through
my house," Aurora recalls. "I thought 'This must be a burglar.'
He was silhouetted against the hall light in the doorway and
he looked like Robert Young in 'Father Knows Best.' I was
cracking up. It was too weird. He was wearing a cashmere
coat and a felt hat and carrying a briefcase. He was doing a
prototype of my favorite man on the planet," she adds giddily.
"The very high level ones have the ability to change form.
Sometimes, if someone has a Catholic orientation, they may
appear as Mother Mary. They appear as whatever you are able
to attune yourself to." Eventually, the intruder "went out the
bedroom window. And that's when I saw the spaceships
across the street in the park." "Yes, yes," I say, "but I don't understand why you think these two incidents were related!
Can't an argument be made that there were spaceships across
the street in the park *and* Robert Young had some sort of
mental collapse and was breaking and entering people's
homes for a period of time? When you were eight was probably when 'Father Knows Best' was going off the air. . . . He
was under a lot of stress . . . career anxiety. . . ." She just
laughs at me. Because I am silly. Aurora knows what she
knows.

Just the way that Michael knows what really happened to

him when he was six and fell off the Oceanside pier as he was walking along with his schoolteacher mother and hypnotist father. When he took the plunge off the railing, instead of taking a direct route to the water, forty feet below, he "was physically transported to the sixth dimensional plane" where he "was taken aboard a spaceship. The human-appearing beings were telepathically telling me that everything was going to be okay. For me, this verified that for those of us who are termed 'star beings,' if we are true to our ideals and principles when we live on this level, we will have intervention. Something outside us will help us." This rings true for Aurora, who nostalgically remembers the time she "was teleported through a time-space warp" when she was sixteen and "about to crash into five lanes of traffic. They moved my whole car to a new location during rush hour." Sadly, no one witnessed this event, which certainly would have been a very cool sight. Just as there were no witnesses to Michael's vanishing act during his fall, because in *both* cases THE HUMAN-APPEARING EXTRA-TERRESTRIALS RETURNED THEM TO THE VERY SAME PRE-DISASTER MOMENT FROM WHENCE THEY DEPARTED!! which certainly explains everything except this:

Why do they bother? Why do they care enough about complete strangers to risk, at the very least, the outer space equivalent of a hernia? "Wouldn't it make sense that a very spiritually and technologically advanced being would want to share that with someone else?" asks Michael. "They're in guardian action around the planet. This is one of the things the world leaders are holding over our heads. They want to make us think that *they* somehow are going to solve all our problems when actually the higher forces would not *allow* them to have a thermonuclear war." (Well, *that's* a relief.)

Since Aurora and Michael began their mission together (their wedding announcement read "The Global confederacy presents the re-uniting in wedded bliss of Lady Aurora and Michael David El Legion") their worldview has expanded to include an awful lot of conspiracy theories having to do with nefarious government forces designing every unfortunate event from the Kennedy assassination to the cold war, the L.A. riots, and even earthquakes. "I believe the government is actually trying to create the quakes," Michael says matter-of-factly, "because that would give them an excuse to exercise martial law. They'd like total control over this area because there are a lot of creative people here who are a threat to the established order."

"But humanity *does* have a lot to look forward to," Aurora adds. "It's not *all* doom and gloom. The men in the white spaceships are coming."

"What has been referred to as 'the rapture' by traditional Christianity is another term for the evacuation phase that's coming," says Michael.

By now my head feels like it's imploding. Maybe because these people do not behave like raving maniacs although Michael does have the intensity of an evangelist possessed by the spirit. So wrapped up is he in providing a listener with documentation for every new twist in his premise that he doesn't notice little saliva balls accumulating in the corners of his mouth. Nevertheless, he is articulate and genteel in his colorful designer sweater, pressed gray slacks, and Italian loafers. Aurora seems every inch the reasonable hostess as she gets up to offer everyone some iced tea. "Most of the people who interview us are star people," Michael tells me, "whether you are aware of it or not. That's why you are drawn to us." Really?

Me? This is certainly nothing I had ever considered before. Even after perusal of a long list of "star people characteristics," I am not aware of being "sensitive to electromagnetic forcefields." I'm not even sure what they are. And I don't think I have "an especially low body temperature," "an unusual blood type," or "paranormal abilities." On the other hand, I *do* have "art, music, acting ability" and "children and animals are attracted" to me. (Well, animals, anyway; or maybe I am the one who is attracted.) I *definitely* "feel a great urgency, a short time to complete an important goal," especially with this book deadline looming. Come to think of it, maybe I *do* "feel like one of the 144,000." I just hope that if a being is on his way to take a walk through my house in the middle of the night to explain my earth mission to me, he knows to go with the form of Mel Gibson. In fact, the sooner the better.

"One of the reasons Aurora and I moved here," Michael adds, "we're going to be involved in the movie industry. Getting the light workers together to help wake up the planet."

Which brings us back to that phone call from Aurora about finding an agent. I'm not sure what to tell her. "Geez," I finally say. "If I had a direct line to Jesus or even Commander Voltra, I think I would ask *them*. In fact, if it's not too much trouble, call me back and let me know what they have to say. Because everyone *I* know in this dimension is floundering and hopelessly confused. None of us can figure the damn thing out."

Who would have thought, in this world of enigmas, that finding an agent may be the one eternal mystery to which even those people who have an explanation for *everything* can find no satisfactory answer.

Curl up in bed with one
of your favorite books.

• • •

AMY FISHER:
MY STORY

Having just finished reading the newly published *Amy Fisher:
My Story,* it occurs to me that one side of this incredibly well
examined saga has yet to be revealed. *My* side.

The book offers a full chronology of the events surrounding
the shooting of Maryjo Buttafuoco. And because I am a meticulous and compulsive keeper of journals, I am able to make
known here—for the first time anywhere—exactly what *my*
activities were on those fateful days in 1991 and '92 that culmi-
nated in Amy Fisher's tragic, misguided attack on the wife of
her then-lover, Joey Buttafuoco.

All of what you are about to read is true. Pathetic—yes—
but true nonetheless.

LATE MAY 1991: AMY brings her car in to Complete Auto Body after she had broken her sideview mirror and begins a flirtation with JOEY BUTTAFUOCO.

During this same period, I am preoccupied with the wide variety of ways my six-month-old, ninety-pound "puppy," Lewis, is able to wreak untold destruction upon my home. The nadir comes on a walk in late May '91 when I learn in a gross but oddly festive way that he has apparently consumed but not thoroughly digested a number of brightly colored party balloons.

JULY 2, 1994: JOEY drives AMY home from the car sound-system installer, asks to see the inside of her house, and they become lovers.

I am involved in a rehearsal at my home with my scene partner from acting class—a brooding, angst-ridden twenty-something "Melrose Place" cast member wannabe. Mid-rehearsal, as he begins flirting with me, he reveals that "I always tell women 'I'm trouble. I'm dangerous. Stay away from me.' " That makes me kind of nervous, but not as nervous as I feel after he adds that "in my last relationship toward the end the police were involved quite a bit." "I feel I am expanding exponentially" he says to me, apropos of nothing, and then wants to know if I would be willing to try one rehearsal where he would tie me up. I begin to think that maybe a new scene partner is a good thing to look into.

MID-SEPTEMBER 1991: At JOEY'S suggestion AMY begins to work at ABBA Escort Agency as a prostitute.

Back at acting class, my *new* scene partner—a buffed-up blond guy who looks and talks like a lifeguard—explains that he would like us to do a scene that involves a lot of sexuality and touching. He then goes on to tell me that because of his fundamentalist Christian upbringing he is having trouble finding girls to date. For instance, he would never date a girl from a divorced family because then they think divorce is an option. I begin to wonder if I wouldn't have been smarter just to sign on with the ABBA escort service myself.

NOVEMBER 1991: AMY tearfully asks JOEY to choose between her and MARYJO. When he refuses she breaks up with him, then slashes her wrists.

I go out on an audition in which I read for the part of a lawyer in a movie called *The Gun in Bettylou's Handbag*. After I finish, the director asks me if I could try reading it again, "only this time do it stupider." I have trouble with this. As I am leaving the room, the director says to me, "I hope you won't take this as an insult, but you're just too smart for the part." And so I drive home alone, depressed, torturing myself about not being able to convince him that I am every bit as stupid as the next person.

JANUARY 1992: After Amy's father has initiated new auto repair work, JOEY recontacts AMY and wins her back. They resume their relationship.

I finally get around to reading *Men Who Can't Love*. I am driven to it by my desire to find an explanation for the very bizarre behavior of a guy I had just begun to date. I am stunned. There is such an in-depth portrait of him in the book's list of "danger signals" that I am surprised they have neglected to include his photograph. If only I had sent my copy of the book to Amy when I was done with it. Maybe everything would have turned out differently.

LATE JANUARY 1992: JOEY asks AMY to join the "Future Physique Gym" so they can work out together. She begins to date Paul Makely as she also takes on some clients privately as a prostitute.

I accept an invitation to a Super Bowl party from a girl in my acting class. Turns out she has invited a guy she is trying to fix me up with and he seems like a nice enough fellow. But then the hostess gets dead drunk and begins to follow me around, interrogating me in a tone of voice that is much much too loud considering the location of the guy, who is always sort of nearby.

"What do you think of him?" she bellows. "I think he likes you. Do you like him? Isn't he gorgeous? He has a very big dick. I fucked him."

I am so mortified that I begin trying to figure out how to disappear and still not hurt anyone's feelings. But it all turns out to be a moot point because as soon as the game itself starts the hostess passes out cold, facedown, on her living room floor. I am able to escape to freedom.

MAY 13, 1992: AMY finds out how to purchase a gun from a guy named Paul G.

I begin to fret about what appears to be the premature demise of a new liaison with a guy who actually asked me out *in the middle of the L.A. riots*. Gee! Who woulda thought that a relationship with a beginning like that might hit a rocky patch eventually?

MAY 20, 1992: AMY shoots MARYJO BUTTAFUOCO.

I have dinner with my friend Carol, who explains to me that the phrase "I'll talk to you soon" is even a bigger kiss-off than "I had a nice time. I'll call you." I have so much to learn.

MAY 21, 1992: AMY is arrested.

We are both questioned. She by police and me by radio personalities that my book publisher has lined up for me to talk to about my first book. AMY changes her story a few times, unsure of what to say, before she finally arrives at the most effective version of her story. So, too, do I finally decide that the best answer to "What are you working on now?" is "The live album. It's a lot of my best-loved hits and a few new tunes that I think will really surprise people."

JUNE 21, 1992: AMY pleads not guilty and her bail is set at two million dollars. Nassau County Assistant District Attorney Fred Klein calls her "totally uncontrollable."

I believe he would have said much the same thing about me if he could have seen me attempting a new Kathy Smith workout tape in my bedroom. Trying to keep up with the complex dance routines, I find myself whirling and slamming into my closets and chairs, a display my dogs find truly terrifying.

JUNE 30, 1992: MARYJO identifies AMY in a police lineup.

I have dinner with a friend who I haven't seen in so long I don't think I could have picked her out of a police lineup. A guy at a nearby table is watching us. Somehow he knows who I am and decides to give me his number, describing himself as "a musician-cremation salesman." True love at last!

AUGUST 14, 1992: The gun AMY used is found.

I have my picture taken for the cover of my new book. Afterward, the photographer and I decide to go out and have sushi. While we are dining, a group of incredibly drunk college boys comes into the restaurant. Desperately scanning the room for unaccompanied women, they eventually spot us. The drunkest among them sends us a note that says "I love you both." It is followed by a note that says "Really. No kidding."

"We love you, too," I say to him. "Thank you so much for sharing with us." Then we pay our check and bolt before we have to witness our new loved one passed out cold on a giant plate of uncooked fish.

AUGUST 23–25, 1992: AMY accepts a plea bargain as PAUL MAKELY betrays her by releasing a secret tape he made of her to the tabloids.

I go up to northern California to help my widower dad pack up for a move out of the family home. In helping him decide what stuff he is going to take to his new apartment, I realize that he is planning to throw away every birthday, Christmas, and Father's Day gift I have ever purchased for him in the last twenty years. Since I always overspent on these gifts in the hopes of impressing him, like AMY I felt a little bit betrayed. If I had only comprehended at the time of purchase that their ultimate fate would be a return trip to *my* home, I would have bought him more dangly earrings and Armani jackets over the years.

SEPTEMBER 26, 1992: AMY attempts suicide and is rushed to the hospital.

I finish helping Dad pack. At the end we go to dinner and have a "talk" during which he says to me, "Maybe you don't *really* want what you *think* you really want." I realize that it is teachings such as these (to say nothing of his now-classic "Let's *go* so we can get *back*") that have made me the insecure, shuddering, bleary-eyed lunatic that I am today. However, unlike AMY, rather than suicide I attempt *Buns of Steel.* And I am delighted to discover that it does not require any dancing.

JANUARY 3, 1993: ABC and CBS air AMY FISHER movies simultaneously.
I fall asleep in the middle of them and have a dream about riding on escalators with space aliens.

Well, I guess only the fullness of time will reveal the complex interconnections between our stories. In the meanwhile, I have a quiet sense of peace knowing you are finally acquainted with *my* side of the story.

Attend a trade show
or convention.

• • •

ONE OF THE MOST
THRILLING DAYS OF MY LIFE

"People never say what they mean," the speaker tells us for
the third time. He is a bug-eyed redhead in his early thirties
named Peter Lowe and he is addressing what looks like a sell-
out crowd of several thousand people who have come to the
L.A. Convention Center to attend "SUCCESS '93. SEE YOU AT
THE TOP!" We are here to learn "How to gain rapport with
anyone . . . instantly!" and "How to turn dreams into reality."
And we are as widely varied a group of humans as I have seen
congregated in one place at one time since high school as-
sembly. The black guy with the gold earring in the gray
sweatshirt looks like a rapper. The woman in front of me in
the dark green sport coat and scruffy half-boots looks like a
riding instructor. The blond woman across the aisle in the
brown turtleneck knit dress and patterned nylons looks like a

kindergarten teacher. The bulldog-faced guy in the tight sport coat seated behind her looks like . . . okay *he* looks like a salesman.

"It was one of the most thrilling days of my life," says Shirley Hartford of Century 21 right at the top of the advertisement that caught my attention in the L.A. *Times.* "What will *you* be saying after attending this dynamic event?" I can't wait to find out. I haven't had that many extraordinarily thrilling days lately. This sounds like something I can't afford to miss.

"Before we begin, I want you to turn to someone you don't know and introduce yourself," says the speaker. Since I have a history of being unwilling to participate even in audience clap-alongs at incredibly cool rock concerts, I am naturally planning to stare at my lap and pretend that I didn't hear the command when the woman seated in front of me turns, fixes me with a direct stare, offers me a hearty handshake, and tells me she is Barbara from Egghead Computer. That's when I remember I am a minority group member here—a spy in the ranks. I am the lone person from the customer sector.

"When we talk to a customer and they come up with an objection, it's a time of stress for us," says the speaker, "But remember, in our society customers are trained to automatically give objections. It's a time of stress for them, too."

This is a new one. The idea that my reluctance to throw out my own money on questionable purchases amounts to stress for salespeople has never occurred to me before. I usually regard salespeople as land mines in a ground war I would rather not fight. When I shop, I don't want to interact with anyone. I don't want to hear how nice I look. I don't want to hear how smart I am or what a wise decision I am making. But I never realized this made me a nightmare to all the people who now surround me here at SUCCESS '93.

"In selling, it's not *what* you know but what you can *think of in time*," the speaker tells us. He encourages us to open up our complimentary booklet ("Yes! You can learn how to sell effectively!") to page two and study the diagrammed hands that are labeled "The Precision Model." "Why do we use the precision model?" it asks on the bottom of the page. "Because PEOPLE NEVER SAY WHAT THEY MEAN."

"*All, every,* and *never* are 'universals,'" says the speaker. "They indicate a loop in the customer's mind. For example, a customer says to you, 'Everyone is buying Japanese cars.' You need to break that loop. So you respond, 'Everyone???' 'Well, I guess not *everyone*,' the customer is forced to admit. Now the loop is broken. Universals are *never* true." ("Never?" I want to yell out.) He's on a roll now. We're getting to the meat of the selling sandwich, so to speak. "Trying harder doesn't work," he tells us. "You know what works? The RMA works. What's the RMA? The Right Mental Attitude. And what feeds the RMA? The RPE. What's the RPE? Recent Positive Experiences."

The guy across the aisle from me blows his nose into a napkin and looks into it as Peter Lowe prepares to reveal the key: THE THREE RULES OF SELLING. He writes a single word on the overhead projector: Rapport. "Rapport. Rapport. Rapport. You *must* establish rapport with your customer," he explains. "How? Communicate based on their feelings. By matching someone's physiology exactly, by matching the tone of their speech, the volume of their speech, the tempo of their speech, you also build a rapport with them. And once you have a rapport, then you can shift into your sales pitch and they will shift with you."

This stuff is starting to make me uneasy. The very idea that there are books, tapes, whole schools of psychological and philosophical strategy designed to coerce me into buying things I don't necessarily want suddenly makes us customers sound like naive victims in a big insidious plot. What recourse is there for the poor, overtaxed, underdefended customer? What schools of thought can we turn to in a brave attempt to hold our own in the face of such an onslaught? Which is why I now offer:

Obstinacy '94. Yes, You Can Learn How to Buy Only What You Want To

1. The single greatest key to holding your own as a customer is NC: No Communication. To do this most effectively you will need to learn the perfect LMAF: The Leave Me Alone Face. You must appear to be a person whose every pore and follicle scream out, "I am a ticking time bomb. All my feelings are just about dead. Don't be the one to trigger the final frightening explosion."

2. If this is not immediately effective, remember that *sales people never mean what they say.* So it will catch them off balance if you question the veracity of their every word. If the salesperson comments "You look very well in that outfit" respond instantly "Compared to what? To how I looked when I came into the shop? Are you saying you didn't like how I looked in what I was wearing when I came in?" They will answer, "No, no, I didn't mean that. I thought you looked very nice." "You did?" you reply, "I thought I looked horrible. Fat and bloated. If you thought *that* looked okay, I can't trust your judgment."

All the while, be sure to Stand By *all* Your Universals (SBYU). For example, if you say "Everyone is buying Japanese cars," and the salesman says "Everyone?" you immediately snap, "Yes, *everyone*. Do you have some difficulty with your hearing? Maybe not everyone in the whole big wide world, but everyone that I know and have any respect for, which is all the people whose judgment matters to me. Now which other of my opinions do you want to pick apart and dispute, Mr. Waiting and Hoping and Praying for a Commission Sales Wizard?"

3. Meanwhile, be sure to watch closely to see if you are being "mirrored." When you lean forward, does your sales person lean forward? When you speak softly, does he? If you sense that this is taking place, begin to behave erratically. Shout in the middle of a sentence. Sit down. Stand up. Spin around for no reason. Lie face down on the counter and begin to sob quietly. Now take out the *Merck Manual* and insist that the sales person help you to diagnose the symptoms that you feel. Does he think you have septicemia, liver tumors, or some kind of nerve damage? Do they have a sphygmomanometer on the premises? This is the moment when you must begin to overwhelm him with your HMA (Horrible Mental Attitude). Remind him of the futility of a frivolous materialistic purchase in a world so full of tragedies as ours. "Sure," you say, "I could start to make endless payments on this giganto TV, but wouldn't it be better if I just donated the whole sum to the

United Nations International Childrens Emergency Fund? Then at least I can write it off on my taxes. Not that I even have any money to spare." Now take out some of your current bills. "Look at this $3,100 Visa bill," you say. By now the salesperson should be wide-eyed, pale, and clammy; a twitching, throbbing, wretched mess. Which is precisely the moment you choose to *close the deal*. "Do you like my watch?" you ask. "I got it as a Christmas present. It's a fifteen-hundred-dollar value but I can let you have it for eight-fifty."

And before you know it, you will leave the store not only without a needless purchase but with pockets full of spending money you didn't expect to have when you came in! Plus the warm glow of satisfaction that comes from knowing you have avenged your fellow customers maybe for the first time ever.

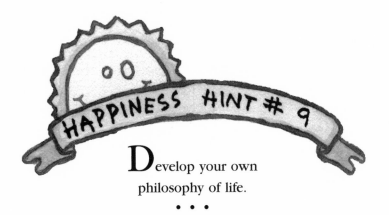

Develop your own
philosophy of life.

• • •

LIFE 102

A book called *Life 101: Everything We Wish We Had Learned
About Life in School—but Didn't* made the best-seller lists a
while ago. Having read it, I think that much of its appeal was
the enticing title, because it seems to me that the authors ignored a lot of the stuff I wish I had learned from *someone*.
Thus, my motivation for writing the following tips. These are
lessons it has taken me a lifetime to learn.

TAKING CONTROL

Can we control anything? Is life just a series of random events,
or is there a plan? In either case, what if anything can we as in-
dividuals do to influence the course of our lives?

The essential nature of the universe is contrary. If you *want* something, you can be sure you will never get it. On the other hand, when you are really trying to *avoid* something, you can be assured that it will come your way. Therefore, the way to make sure you get what you want is to remember to hate what you love. Then you will get what you hoped for. You just won't be able to tell anyone about it.

This works in a wide variety of ways and is at the root of why we are able to control the weather through the use of inappropriate clothing. By this I mean that in order to *guarantee* that the weather will be very hot, a person need only dress in extremely heavy clothes that cannot be removed in layers. Conversely, it is almost a given that wearing extremely light-weight garments—the flimsier the better—will result in weather that's damp and blustery.

What we must learn from all of this is: the only way to make absolutely sure that things will go the way we want them to is to try and screw them up on purpose. If you purposely *try* to make mistakes, perfection will be the result.

Being a Woman

Finding "the makeup shade that's just right for your skin tone!" or "the haircut that's perfect for your face shape" or even learning all "ten terrific new ways to tighten your tummy" will still not help you look even a little bit more like the girls in the diet-cola ads. This is because the girls in the diet-cola ads are often *13 years old.* Even they are not going to look like the girls in the diet-cola ads in a couple of months. And so the only way to deal with your female vanity in our society is to remember this important truth: *Mirrors lie. You are much better looking than that in 3-D.*

MEN

Men are completely nuts. Women can't understand their behavior because men themselves have no clue as to what they are doing or why. However, there is one incredibly important thing to watch for in the early stages of getting to know a man that will give you all the real information you will need. Men almost always feel compelled to announce their personal deficiencies. The mistake that women make is *we don't believe them*. Learning to listen for a man's usually accurate self-assessment can save a woman a great deal of time and guesswork. If a man tells you that he is a jerk and he doesn't think he is ready to make a real commitment, *believe him*. Spending a couple of months with you is *not* going to be the magical catalyst that will change him. And he almost definitely is not going to go into therapy. Men, as a general rule, shy away from therapy because there is no obvious way to keep score. Other danger signals are:

Excessive charm. Men who have a lot of charm have it in place of something real that you are eventually going to want from them and find that they do not have. It is wise to remember that quite a few of our recent mass murderers have been cute guys. Somewhere, some stupid woman probably called up her friend and said, "Ted Bundy hasn't called me in two days. Do you think *I* should call *him*?"

Fast walking. I don't mean fast walking. I mean walking half a block ahead of you, no matter how fast you walk, and never slowing down to accommodate you. An informal poll I have been taking for quite a number of years has convinced me that these fast-walking guys also have terrible tempers and commitment problems. If you don't believe me, ask a friend of yours who is seeing someone with a terrible temper and a history of cheating whether or not her man walks half a block ahead of her and prepare to be amazed.

Dating

Because of what we learned earlier about the essential nature of the universe, it only stands to reason that the more you prepare for a date, the more disappointing the date will turn out to be. In fact, the surest way to make a date cancel or disappear entirely is to go out and buy yourself some sexy, expensive new underwear. And while we're on this topic, it is wise to remember that although many of those underwear get-ups look fetching on the models in the catalog, most of them have the potential to make an otherwise fit and attractive female human suddenly turn into someone who looks like one of the dancing ballerina hippos from *Fantasia*.

One last bit of warning: there is a definite correlation between a man's gift giving and the longevity of the relationship. The more impressive the quantity and quality of gift items early on, the less impressive the chances for the future of the relationship. It's like the guys with charm. Men who supplement early dating with a lot of swell gifts and prizes are generally distracting you from the stuff they are never going to give you.

Television

There will never be anything good on to watch when you need there to be. Ever. In any of our lifetimes.

SHOPPING

• The stuff on the aisles costs *more* than the stuff in the middle.

• Shoes that almost fit when you try them on will not suddenly get comfy a few weeks later. They will always *almost fit* until they drive you insane.

• Any store with the word *classy* in the name can never be. This goes double if it's spelled with a *k*.

• By the time you decide to buy a trendy item, only the out-of-it people will be wearing it.

EATING

There are four basic food groups: salad, hors d'oeuvres, pasta, and diet drinks. It is appropriate to eat from two of these groups per meal. If you are the sort of person who always thinks she needs to go on a diet, realize this: *everything will always make you fat for the rest of your life*. This is especially true if you live with someone who never gains weight. It is due to a little-known phenomenon called Secondary-Weight Gain, which operates in the same manner as Secondary-Smoke Inhalation. In other words, calories are calories and they have to go somewhere—meaning that *you* will somehow assimilate and convert into fat all the calories that are going unassimilated by perpetually thin people. You get your calories *and* their calories, thus causing you to mysteriously gain weight even when you eat only carrots.

Safety

They only *real safe* day of any given time period is the day (or days) on which Nostradamus—or the Cal Tech Seismology Lab—has predicted an earthquake. It is the only day on which you can count on nothing happening at all.

Conclusions

As we whiz by on this exhilarating and often nauseating tilt-a-whirl experience we call life, it's important to live in the *now*. And if the now seems to be racing by too quickly, go out to a beach or a mall or a gym and find a very attractive man. Introduce yourself, chat for a while, and then give him your phone number and ask him to call you. Suddenly you will experience sixty-hour days.

P amper yourself with a
day of beauty.

• • •

My Year of Health and Beauty for *You!*

People have always said to me, "Merrill, share your beauty secrets with us." Yes, they are imaginary people, but if you prick
them do they not bleed? Well, no, because they are imaginary
people. But I believe that real people might clamor for this advice as well if they ever dreamed I had it to give. And, after all,
why not me? What good does it do the average beauty seeker
to get advice from Cindy Crawford or Christie Brinkley? These
are women who were born genetically perfect. What useful
hints can they possibly have to share besides, "Next time you
are born, try to get better-looking parents."

A few years ago Christie Brinkley published a beauty-and-
fitness book in which she gave the following advice:
"Moisturize! Moisturize! Moisturize!" I don't want to imply that
her approach may have been too simplistic, but perhaps she

herself wound up overly moistened because recent supermarket tabloids report that at thirty-nine years old she is already having plastic surgery. See what I mean? Might as well take your advice from me. What have you got to lose?

CHAPTER 1

Skin: Thank God for Skin!

If it weren't for our good friend skin, this would have been a chapter on skeleton maintenance. And if you think fingernail maintenance is a nuisance, imagine all the bleaching, sanding, varnishing, painting, wrapping, caulking, buffing, and beveling there would be in order to care for and dress all those bones. On the plus side, I guess weight control would become a moot point. And runway modeling agencies would suddenly be equal opportunity employers. But we might as well stop our daydreaming and face the truth: Skin is here to stay for the foreseeable future.

There are two basic approaches to skin care:

Skin care for women

For women, there is a very high premium placed on being facially moist. Toward this end, every woman is expected to purchase and apply a wide variety of specialty moisturizers. There is one for the skin *under* the eye only to be worn at night, and another one for the same area during the day. There are over-all facial moisturizers to be worn under street makeup and other ones specifically for bedtime. Scientific laboratories are working around the clock on the daunting task of helping to keep the faces of women everywhere perpetually damp, so it is not reasonable to be discouraged by the fact that there is still no proof that not one of the preparations currently available does anything to retard or reverse the aging process. Just because they don't appear to have worked for Christie Brinkley doesn't mean they won't work for you. Maybe she was just too genetically perfect to reap the potential benefits. Yes! That's probably the reason! After all, we always suspected there had to be a down side to looking that great. So go ahead and slather the stuff on regardless.

Skin care for men

The approach here is slightly less complex. In the event of caking or clumping of mud, hose off. Towel dry.

Wrinkle Prevention

The best advice I have heard on this subject comes from the actress Morgan Fairchild, who, in a women's-magazine interview, revealed her patented method of "smiling downward" to reduce laugh lines and crow's feet. As you practice this, you may find that some people will call you "lizard face." Let them go right ahead. It's a small price to pay because even if you do develop wrinkles over the course of time, everyone will be so distracted by your odd reptilian facial expressions that they will probably not even notice. The last thing on their minds will be whether or not you had wrinkles.

Makeup the Merrill Way: The Raccoon

Many pages have been written on the classic ways to apply cosmetics with skill and artistry. Generally, the approach seems to be fleshtones for the face and neck, primary colors for the lips and eyelids. Except, of course, in a circus or carnival environment, in which it is usually just the reverse.

The really challenging part of wearing makeup is the hourly maintenance. No matter how carefully a woman applies her makeup initially, the next time she checks most of it will have changed locations or disappeared entirely. This is precisely why, when I developed *my* beauty plan, I looked to one of nature's cleverest and most lovable creatures: the raccoon.

To achieve this look, prepare the eyes in the traditional manner, applying multiple coats of mascara, pencil, liner, powder, and shadow. Now check yourself in the mirror. Perfect! Except for the way your eye kind of itches. Notice how it's already beginning to tear. Don't resist. Go ahead. Indulge. Give in to it willingly. The resulting dark makeup circles will not only give you "the look of the raccoon," but they will last day and night for up to forty-eight hours. In fact, just try to get them off!

Hair Care

There are a number of different approaches to hair care.

Former Charlie's Angel Jaclyn Smith explains *her* approach this way in *The American Look by Jaclyn Smith*: "Each time I emerge from the shower I have several distinct options before me. I can choose from a gamut of contemporary styles." I must respond to her, "Well, well, well, aren't you little miss Hair Queen of the Universe." It has never worked remotely like that for me. I explain *my* approach this way: Each time I emerge from the shower, I have the same single distinct option before me. Sure, I can *choose* from a gamut of contemporary styles, but no matter what I select, I will be seen later that day sporting the same medium-length, fine, straight brown hair that has been attached to my head, resisting styling, in every photo of me ever taken since I was two years old. So, doesn't it make very good sense that each time I emerge from the shower, I *choose* fine, medium-length, straight brown hair as my style? I suggest you take a look at your own baby photos and decide that will be the style for *you.*

Wardrobe: Pink—A Color Just for You!

Traditional wisdom tells us that it is advisable to organize your wardrobe around one or two basic colors, the better to maximize your ability to mix and match. This is precisely why there is only one color for the overworked, frantic, confused fashion follower: Pink! The same color that all of your clothes are going to be anyway after that one crazed, distracted evening when you forget to separate the white clothes from the colored ones when you're doing the wash. Relax. From now on, do it that way any time you like. Once you have embraced pink as your color, everything you own becomes a part of one gigantic ensemble. If you need to accent with an additional color, I suggest gray—the color everything else has probably turned by now as well.

Now relax and stop worrying about how you look. Everything is fine. Use the time you will save to help figure out this whole federal budget crisis thing. And if you happen to come up with anything good, tell them you have no choice but to share the credit with me.

Push your sense of romance
to the next level.

• • •

BLIND DATE

WITH THE UNIVERSE

Like a lot of women in the greater Los Angeles area, I have
been to see a psychic and I'm not ashamed to admit it. Okay,
I'm *kind of* ashamed to admit it. But not all that ashamed.
That's one of the advantages of living in southern California. A
whole lot of shame is not really required about anything.

There was a time when I enjoyed paying someone whose
only qualification might be the ability to purchase and operate
a neon sign for the privilege of hearing great news about my
incredible future. It seemed to me that being able to pay someone to tell you that everything was going to be okay was a particularly wonderful service to have at your disposal. Right up
until the day when a thirtyish lady doing readings at a card table in Malibu decided to tell me that someone in my life would
die in September. "Definitely September," she said to me. "If

not this year, then next year. Guaranteed within a year." And I paid her twenty dollars for this? After I sweated through three completely terrifying Septembers (I threw in an extra one out of panic) during which no one died, I decided this was not a service I would pay for again. After all, another nice thing about living in Los Angeles is that catastrophic news is available at absolutely no cost twenty-four hours a day.

So that was it for me and psychic predictions until last week, when I decided to include a psychic in a piece I was doing about the upcoming national elections. She was sitting in a small building decorated with slightly spooky paintings of wizards and planets. "George Bush is going to lose," she said to me, "definitely." Then she looked at me quizzically. "Are you going to be in the East any time soon?" she asked. As a matter of fact, I had tickets to go to the East Coast at the end of that very week. So I said, "Yes." "Are you aware of the man in your life?" she asked me. "Uh . . . I don't know. I don't think so," I said. "You have 'relationship' all over your vibes," she said to me. "Get ready. You will meet a man in the East."

I was laughing out loud when I left her strange little building. The whole thing amused me big time until a few days later when I began packing for my trip to New York. She *had* gotten the election results right, I thought to myself. And that *was* pretty good about me going to the East. She pulled that one out of nowhere. I didn't give her any clues. I hadn't even been in a very good mood when I talked to her, so these darn relationship vibes she was picking up must be pretty powerful. Could it be, perhaps, because they were part of A LOVE THAT WAS DESTINED TO BURN THROUGH THE PAGES OF HISTORY??? Or CAPTURE THE IMAGINATION OF A GENERATION??? Maybe I'd better rush out and buy some new underwear. Luckily for me I remembered, at the last minute, that buying new underwear is a violation of one of the foremost precepts of the laws of romantic love: The greater the pre-date preparation, the worse the actual date. So I did the bravest thing of all: absolutely nothing.

As I drove to the airport I became aware of a certain level of nervous tension that struck me as somehow familiar. Gradually I recognized it. It was blind date jitters. I felt like I was on a blind date with the universe.

It was not pleasant. I really hate blind dates. I've only ever been on one, but it was a memorable bummer. On that occasion, Michael, a handsome, talented friend of mine (who is married to Polly, an equally impressive girlfriend of mine), decided to introduce me to one of his friends. Because I liked Michael so much, it seemed like a good set of odds. However, because I think I'm the queen of the incredibly accurate split-second snap judgment, from the moment I laid eyes on date boy I just wanted to be at home by myself doing pretty much anything else. Suddenly it seemed like the perfect time to get down to some serious mildew removal in the garage, which I'd been meaning to do for about eight years.

To be fair, the guy never did or said anything that terrible. It was the tension underlying the entire premise that I found unbearable. So when the evening finally wheezed to a close, I gave him a hearty handshake, thanked him warmly for the wonderful time, and then got into my car embalmed in self-pity and drove off to purchase powerful anesthetizing beverages.

To make matters worse, for the next few weeks I could tell that my friends felt weird about the whole thing. Michael took it kind of personally that I hadn't cared for his buddy. Hoping to patch things up, he and Polly and I all went out to dinner a few weeks later. Doing my best to appear the very picture of affable good nature, I looked sweetly up at him over a plate of recently deceased shellfish and asked, "So! How's that friend of yours doing?"

"Oh, him," he replied. "I guess I didn't tell you. He stole a bunch of stuff from me, so I had him arrested."

From that point forward my definition of a blind date has been this: a tension-filled occasion upon which your dear close friends force you to dine out with felons.

So, as I boarded the plane for New York, I felt myself growing increasingly anxious. This was, after all, an aircraft full of people with whom I was destined to be in the East, many of whom were men. I scanned the plane carefully. No one looked particularly interesting to me. What exactly were the rules of this anyway? Did that mean that *he* wasn't in here? Or was I suddenly living in a "Gilligan's Island" where I would be forced to share THE LOVE THAT ROCKED A NATION with one of these guys, whether I liked him or not? Or was this like *A Midsummer Night's Dream* and did I now have some kind of wacky power that could generate passion in pretty much anyone I made the mistake of gazing at too fondly?

A huge oatmeal-colored lime-scented biker guy sat down in the seat beside me. It seemed too risky even to say hello, so I reached into the seat pocket in front of me and pretended to carefully study the colorful diagrams of the emergency exits, both in Spanish and in English. I was tremendously relieved when he immediately fell into a lumplike snoring slumber from which he never awakened for the duration of the flight, not even to enjoy his tiny pack of complimentary almonds. I had to be very careful.

When we landed at JFK Airport, my scrutinizing got even more manic. Suddenly every man in New York City seemed like a possibility and therefore a threat.

"That one's a nut," the inner narrative went, "Don't look at him. *Or* him. He's scary. Don't make eye contact. Especially not with that one. I don't care who he is, I am not having THE LOVE THAT BURNED THROUGH TIME with a guy who wears multicolored shower clogs."

I hardly spoke to my cab driver. When I got to the hotel I carried my own bag to my room to avoid the bellman. There was an attractive guy on the elevator but I purposely ignored him because he was wearing a wedding ring and I just don't need that kind of grief. For the next twenty-four hours, every time someone said, "Merrill, I'd like you to meet . . ." I'd jump. Then I'd turn my head verrrrry slowly . . . trying to buy a little extra time before my deadly relationship vibes did too much damage.

Actually, I met mostly women.

I cannot tell you how happy I was to get back to L.A., where no prophesied scenario awaited me. That was when I realized how great it is that no one really *can* predict the future. The idea of going through the motions in someone else's script is too unappealing for words. *Especially* when it comes to A LOVE THAT STUNNED A NATION. The way I see it, if I'm going to fall for a felon, I at least want to pick him out myself.

HAPPINESS HINT # 12

Do something you've always
secretly wanted to do.

• • •

A Tour of the
Movie Stars' Homes

The Los Angeles area offers many unique ways to waste time,
but the sky is *really* the limit for people who have a high hu-
miliation threshold. What other population center has a major
metropolitan newspaper whose classified ads are filled with
pleas for television game show participants?

However, of all the things to which you can voluntarily subject yourself, my own personal selection for the winner of the
sleazy recreational activity sweepstakes—and remember, it's
an honor just to be nominated—is A TOUR OF THE MOVIE
STARS' HOMES. Thank you. Thank you very much. I'm sure
your favorites were very sleazy as well.

You don't have to be in Los Angeles for very many consecutive hours before you begin to encounter your options for
such a tour. For starters, there are the little mom-and-pop

card-table map stands set up at dozens of corners along Sunset Boulevard in Beverly Hills that offer for sale not just instructions for a self-guided tour but the only opportunity you may ever get to have a map-reading fight that involves the name and address of Ricky Schroder. Then there are the assorted bus and limousine tours you can board with a group of strangers, perfect for those who do want to meet the other members of a club that would have you for a member. Quite frankly I have always been hesitant to spend that kind of time with people whose greatest desire is to catch a fleeting glimpse of Buddy Hackett. Which is why it wasn't until I became aware of the self-guiding audiocassette car tour that I even for one second considered participating in any of these things myself. Even though it had occurred to me from time to time that maybe having a snobby attitude about this legendary Los Angeles tourist attraction was tantamount to being a New Yorker who refuses to take the ferry out to the Statue of Liberty or appear on a talk show to recount anecdotes about Joey Buttafuoco. So I purchased "The California Cassette Driving Tour of the Movie Stars' Homes," and I now feel qualified to say that it is impossible to imagine a more thoroughly irritating way to spend the day. I say this as someone who was once locked for several hours in the bathroom of a bus.

The cassette is hosted by Doug Llewellyn, the unpleasant little insect who hangs around outside the "People's Court" demoralizing litigants, and a woman named Eileen Conn, whose attempts to engage him in banter are so unfortunate that it took only two or three minutes for me to nominate them both for my permanent lifetime achievement award for the People

I Would Most Like to Strangle with a Garden Hose (and once again, remember that it's an honor just to be nominated).

So come with me now back to those halcyon days of last weekend when I was voluntarily a prisoner in my own car, driving nervously around other people's neighborhoods as I pursued:

MY TOUR OF THE MOVIE STARS' HOMES
(A DRAMATIZATION)

Dear Diary,

Here I am at the specified location near Santa Monica Boulevard and Rodeo Drive in Beverly Hills. Although it is a nice sunny day I saw no reason to change out of my ratty sweat clothes because I knew I was going to be too embarrassed to ever set foot out of the car. I am accompanied by my dog Bo, who is sitting bolt upright beside me in the front seat . . . not because I *wanted* him to join me, but because he escaped from my front yard as I was pulling out of the driveway and I was too lazy to drive him back to the house.

I begin the cassette, which doles out my driving instructions as I proceed. "Be an alert and considerate driver and keep a look out for the stars," chirps Doug Llewellyn. "You never know where they'll turn up." "Ooooh, there's one!" gushes his friend Eileen. "Oh, sorry, Doug. That's just you." Although it is not even noon yet, already I feel my mood starting to sink. I'm beginning to contemplate my own mortality, always a bad sign. But hey! It's a nice day out! It's much too soon to throw in the towel! So, let's take an attitude adjustment and . . . here we go, down one of the many broad, handsome boulevards of Beverly Hills, to our first location, which is . . . hmmm. The unremarkable-looking former residence of the not-too-recently deceased Jimmy Durante. Okay. We're parked here in front. Let's try to get into this. It's kind of an unremarkable-looking structure. The lawn is alive. The shrubs are doing okay. "He was called 'The Old Schnozzola,' " says Doug Llewellyn, launching in to a summary of Jimmy Durante's career that contains only the data about Jimmy Durante that I already know. I guess that's what happens. You entertain millions, you think maybe your life means something, then you die and some miserable weenie like Doug Llewellyn turns you into a boring cliché. "Mrs. Durante still lives here," chirps Doug. She must be in her eighties. That has to be trying enough without having to look out your front window at cars full of pale, bug-eyed strangers slowly cruising by, pointing, in the midst of a map-reading fight. This is too depressing. I've got to get out of here. But wait. I can't leave yet. I don't have instructions to my next destination. Oh good. There's that annoying porno-movie-style jazz soundtrack indicating that we're off. On our way to . . .

"Two thirds of the way up the next block," drones Doug as he regales us with more amazing insider data. Apparently this Beverly Hills is a city full of expensive homes owned by very wealthy people! And here we are at . . . the former residence of Ray Bolger. Another dead guy.

More nice shrubs. Another nice enough lawn. I don't know much about him except that he was the Scarecrow in *The Wizard of Oz* . . . which, of course, is the very thing that Doug would like to tell me. But there's more! Apparently Buddy Ebsen was *almost* cast as the Scarecrow until "he developed a serious allergy to the makeup." "Too bad," says that wacky

Eileen, "I hear he was really *itching* to play the part."
Uh-oh . . . here comes those mortality thoughts again, and this
time they're dragging with them some terror about our hollow
crumbling society. I look over at Bo. Apparently my negativity
is contagious. I see that glistening thing happening around his
nose, an early warning sign of impending car sickness. Hang
on there, pal, I tell him, we're about to move on. We're taking
in some fresh air.

Uh-oh . . . Oh God. It's too late. He's starting to throw up.
Right in front of the home of "the maestro of 'The Love Connection,' Chuck Woolery." That "Chuck has made the Love
Connection himself and lives here with his wife and daugh-
ters" seems to be no comfort to Bo, who is heaving his guts
out in my front seat. Damn! I think I have a towel in my trunk.
But to get it means I have to get out of my car. I hope the maestro isn't watching. Maybe this is a sign that it's time to scratch
the tour and head on home. But on the other hand, I've been
at this less than an hour. I really haven't given it much of a
chance. I'll try just one more location.

Hmm. Another pleasant ranch-style home which is . . . oh,
spit it out!! . . . Yikes. "This is the home of Carl Reiner." *Carl
Reiner! Wait a minute! I know Carl Reiner! And, oh, my God!
There he is! Getting out of his car in his garage!* I don't want
him to see me dressed like a bag lady, sitting in a car still
damp from dog vomit, parked *uninvited in his driveway!* Oh,
no! He's headed this way! It looks like he's going for a walk!
What if he sees me? What'll I tell him? "Hi, Carl. I was just in
the neighborhood to . . . uh . . . visit Ray Bolger. Then I remembered that he's dead so I stopped by to say hello to the
Woolerys and . . ." *Geez! I've got to get out of here!!!*

On my way out of the neighborhood I did see a male and

a female member of the gardening staff of the Peter Falk residence making out on the front porch. And that's a memory I will always cherish.

But for future reference, as far as sleazy recreational activities go, at least the game show tapings offer a chance to win cash.

HAPPINESS HINT # 13

Conduct a meeting with all the members of your household.

• • •

GREETING DISORDER

One afternoon, having arrived home in a bad mood after a long series of thankless chores, it occurred to me that it was time to confront my dogs about an issue between us that was building to insurmountable proportions. I called for the two largest ones, Lewis and Tex, to join me in my office. Since they never come when I call, the two others arrived. I locked them in there and cornered Lewis and Tex in the front room, where we finally thrashed the whole thing out.

ME: Okay, you two, LISTEN CAREFULLY. In the future it is neither necessary nor desirable for you to greet me every single time I walk in the door. Unless a minimum of two hours has passed, the previous greeting is still in effect. In other words, if I come IN the door, and you greet me, and then several minutes later I go OUT the door, only to return in a matter of seconds, you do NOT have to greet me again.

LEWIS: Ha-ha. Good one.

ME: I am serious. Maybe it would be best at this point to discuss the PURPOSE of a greeting.

TEX: What is she talking about?

LEWIS: Play along. We don't eat for about an hour.

ME: A GREETING is what you give someone you have not seen IN A WHILE. A WHILE is a period of time of more than two hours. Try another example. I come in the door after a day of work . . .

TEX: I would be so glad to see you that I would rush up and hurl myself at you. Then I would get up on my back legs, knocking you over, causing you to drop whatever you were carrying . . .

LEWIS: Listen to what you're saying, bro. You know we're not supposed to get UP on her.

ME: Very good, Lewis. Thank you.

LEWIS: Which is why the approach *I* take is to circle closely, using body blocks. Throwing my whole weight against her legs so that she falls over and drops everything. Same exact result. I never have to get UP on her at all.

ME: You're missing the point. All that is required from a greeting is a simple show of enthusiasm. Eyes filled with a certain amount of joy, a bit of tail-wagging. THAT'S IT.

TEX: What did she say?

LEWIS: Just go with it. She likes to hear herself talk.

ME: Now that we've defined a greeting . . .

LEWIS: And by the way, I like to make mine last until she's down on her knees, if not flat on her back . . .

TEX: I've seen your work, buddy. You're an artist.

ME: . . . Let's try one more exercise to see if you are getting the point. Okay. Imagine this. I decide to take out the garbage. I walk to the door . . .

LEWIS: I'm right there with you.

TEX: I beat you there.

LEWIS: The hell you do.

ME: I exit. About eight seconds later I come back *in* the door. What would be your response?

TEX: I'd be so thrilled to see you that I'd run up to you, hurl myself at you, then I'd get up on my back legs and . . .

LEWIS: Dolt. You don't listen. We just went through this a second ago. It's circle and hurl, circle and lean . . . and hurl. Circle and hurl.

ME: STOP! Listen to me! The point was that you do not have to greet me again. You just greeted me seconds before. I'm sorry if this seems confusing but I'd like you just to blindly accept this rule and obey it. DO NOT GREET ME EVERY TIME I COME IN THE DOOR.

LEWIS: So you're asking us to be rude.

TEX: No, no, I hear you. Tell me if I've got it straight. You go OUT the door, and then you come RIGHT BACK IN. We do NOT get up on you. No. We circle and hurl, circle and lean and hurl . . .

LEWIS: There you go. Step on her feet and trip her. Tangle her up, and lean on her and at the same time circle . . .

TEX: I can definitely do that.

LEWIS: Where is she going?

TEX: Looks like the bedroom. Whoa. She closed the door. How long is she going to be gone?

LEWIS I don't know. All I know is suddenly we're very alone.

TEX: How long has it been since we saw her?

LEWIS: I don't know. A month? A year?

TEX: Wait! The door is opening. Oh my God! She's back!

LEWIS: Dear God, thank you! She's back! Welcome back!

TEX: Come let me get up on you and give you a nice big kiss.

HAPPINESS HINT # 14

For at least a weekend, don't answer your phone.

• • •

After the Beep

I like to think of myself as the kind of basic no-nonsense person who doesn't need a lot of fancy schmancy equipment to get by. There's not a shred of evidence that I *am* that sort of person, but I like to think of myself that way.

However, not even in my most feverish delusional fantasies can I imagine having to live a whole day without my answering machine. I am so symbiotically attached to it that I ought to just take the final step and give it a name, the way B. B. King did with his guitar Lucille. Right now I'm thinking of something short and practical. Like Mindy. Or Keith.

My attachment goes beyond the disturbing obsession I've developed with changing my outgoing message almost daily. That's probably pathetic enough. My *real* addiction—the one that holds me in its grip like a tick on a sleeping dog—is the incredible, unbeatable luxury of being permitted to screen my calls. For the past few years the number of times that I have actually had to pick up the phone blindly are so few that I think if I were suddenly forced to go back to doing it on a regular basis it would have such a profound effect on my body chemistry that it might set in motion a series of molecular mishaps that would eventually cause the earth to come loose from its orbit and begin hurtling toward the sun.

Thanks to my dear friend the answering machine I have been permitted to painlessly nip in the bud many potentially irritating interactions well before they have been permitted to blossom and flower into hellish nightmares. Oh sure, there were one or two people who wormed through because of a temporary equipment malfunction. But on the whole, I owe my answering machine a real debt of gratitude. (In fact, now I'm starting to think it deserves a more happening, contemporary name. Something along the lines of Keanu.)

It also has provided me with a kind of X-ray service, as I have noticed that it is possible to tell a great deal about people from the way they sound when they leave a message. If you listen carefully, everything is audible: nervousness, hidden anger or depression, deceit, weasel vibes (come to think of it, with calls like that coming in no wonder I got so hooked on screening).

I don't know if bad answering machine messages have become legal grounds for divorce in the state of California yet, but they have clearly begun to play a significant role in the compendium of macabre behavior that constitutes love in the 1990s. A female friend of mine was so revolted by what she described as "a particularly cutesy outgoing message" that it became a critical element in her decision to have nothing more to do with the guy who recorded it. In a similar vein, the creation and recording of just such a cutesy message put the final nail in the coffin of a shaky relationship for a male friend of mine when it came to pass that his then-girlfriend tried to enlist his participation in an adorable two-person "aren't we a cute couple" exchange she was hoping to record.

I'm not the only person who has been giving too much thought to matters such as these. My friend Billy Kimball astonished me recently by reciting an amazingly evolved theory he called "the five ages of answering machine messages."

"Age one was back when the answering machine was new and involved very meticulous explanations of how the equipment worked," he told me, "such as 'This is not me speaking. You have reached my answering machine. This is a recording. I am not actually here.' Age two, which began after everyone relaxed a bit, involved elaborate, funny messages such as the pre-produced tape you could buy in which someone sang 'Nobody's home! Nobody's home' to Beethoven's Fifth. Age three was born as a reaction to age two and therefore produced a swing to the other extreme resulting in very compressed, terse messages such as 'You know what to do' and 'Leave it.' " In age four, which Billy personally feels is the worst age of all, "the answering machine owner tried to create messages that would help them stake a claim to being an interesting person."

"For some reason," he went on, "they felt compelled to pass along a lot of unneeded information about themselves," "the incoherent babblings of their small children" or "long, barely audible passages of music that are somehow significant." "A lot of girls seemed to do a kind of performance art," he added, citing someone he knows who recorded a combination of music and cackling.

Which brings us to the present, and age five—postmodern. "Here we see people so answering-machine savvy that they are working in parody of form," he went on. Like the one guy we both know who re-records the *same message* on his machine *every day*. Or like some of my own messages, which often say things like "I'm not here right now, which, of course, is a euphemism for 'I'm sitting eight feet away screening calls.' " (And what does Billy have on *his* answering machine? "Hi, I'm in the shower. Leave a message after the tone," which Billy feels is postmodern because it's been on far too long to be true.)

So, now that I've established that the answering machine is a friend to the modern neurotic, the question still remains, "What kind of a friend? Is it a *good* friend?" Well, consider the case of the woman I know whose answering machine decided one day to become an unexpected instrument of karma by suddenly malfunctioning in such a way that it played back her incoming messages randomly to anyone who phoned her house, eventually passing along the details of an affair she was having to the boyfriend behind whose back it was taking place.

I myself have been sitting in my living room with someone when the screening mechanism of my machine began broadcasting gossip about that very person spoken by a third party who had no way of knowing that person could possibly be listening. Talk about an area of etiquette Letitia Baldrige needs to take a look at. What exactly is appropriate behavior in such a circumstance? Do you dive for the machine and tackle it, knowing it's already too late to make amends? Or do you do as I did and suddenly appear to be suffocating from lack of oxygen, then wake up hours later claiming to have amnesia?

And then there's the way the machine plays dumb and just sits there and lets anyone at all simply use it to vent his rage. What kind of a friend would allow that? "I left thirteen nasty screaming messages in a row in one half-hour," a guy I know confessed about the final days of a painful breakup.

In fact, one time someone filled up almost an entire side of *my* tape with a seemingly endless series of *fuck you*s.

Which brings us to the peculiar notion of answering machine as competitor. Because it's obvious that on some occasions people call *hoping* that the machine will pick up. I have done that when I was the bearer of unpleasant news. But then there's the case of the guy I was seeing who seemed to be having *much* better sex with my answering machine than he ever offered when I showed up. And to think I was starting to think of the damn thing as a member of the family. No toaster ever made a grab for one of my boyfriends. To hell with giving it a name. I ought to put it in the garage. Except if I did that, how would I screen my calls?

HAPPINESS HINT # 15

Think up a creative way
to celebrate a special occasion.

• • •

DERANGED LOVE MUTANTS:
THE STORY OF ROMEO AND JULIET

Every year when Valentine's Day rolls around, I make a special point of trying to scan the horizon for a reasonable
example of romantic love, just so I know what we're all supposed to be celebrating.

Of course, the preceding 364 days I am adrift in a sea of stories about love gone dopey. I refer here to both the whining
weepy anecdotes of my various friends as well as those of the
never-ending parade of deranged love mutants booked in
triplicate on the afternoon talk shows. To say nothing of the
stream of stunning examples reported daily.

My favorite:

A 71-year-old woman was arrested Friday after she
allegedly doused her husband of more than 30 years

with rubbing alcohol and set him on fire for eating a chocolate Easter bunny she had saved for herself, police said.

Proving once and for all that when evaluating the success of a love relationship, the element of longevity should not necessarily be the key.

But if *that* isn't, what is? It has become increasingly disturbing how few good models of love there are.

This year, we can't look to the First Couple for any hints. It's pretty apparent that Hillary is just putting the best face on some kind of marital sciatica. In fact, these past few years every single public couple who ever looked the least bit intriguing bought a ticket for the long slow ride to hell.

I still remember with a shudder when I thought Woody and Mia looked like they had worked out something impressive. Eccentric, yes, but romantic and mature. That was way back in the late eighties—when we used to be able to count on England's royal couples to at least fake a show of romance.

This year, we can't even count on Tom and Roseanne. Yes, John Tesh and Connie Selleca would *like* to step up to the plate as our new romantic ideal, but having survived the taping of an embarrassing infomercial is *not* qualification enough.

So this year, in honor of Valentine's Day, I decided to reread a true classic—*Romeo and Juliet.*

If you have not had the occasion to do so lately, please allow me to reacquaint you with the details of this timeless model of romantic love.

When we first meet the teenage Romeo, it is a Sunday night and he has decided to crash a ball just to catch a glimpse of Rosaline, a girl with whom he is desperately in love. Instead, he meets the thirteen-year-old Juliet. And even though, only seconds before he was deeply in love with Rosaline, *now* he knows *instantly* that this thirteen-year-old girl is the greatest love of his life. Really. She is. He's not kidding this time.

Juliet has never been in love before. And yes, their two families hate each other. But so what? My parents never liked anyone I went out with either. The important thing is that by Monday afternoon, so beautiful is their love, they go ahead and get married.

Just one day later.

In lieu of a honeymoon, Romeo kills Juliet's cousin and Juliet goes back home to spend the night at her parents' house. Of course her parents do not know about the marriage yet, but they are so beside themselves with grief about the murdered cousin that Juliet's father decides there is no time like the present to arrange for Juliet to marry an older man.

Well, she *is* thirteen and not getting any younger. Soon, she'll be thirteen and a half. However, because he's an adult and not a hot-headed teenager, he really doesn't want to rush things. So he sets the wedding date for Thursday.

Naturally, the already-married Juliet realizes she must defy her father's wishes. She is no longer a co-dependent. She has boundaries and as a fully *individualized* adult, she must stand up to him and tell him her intentions. She takes the most sensible course of action under the circumstances. She pretends to be dead.

This also bodes very well for the future of her marriage to Romeo since we now know that the core of any "love-at-first-sight" attraction is usually "repetition compulsion"—wherein a person reenacts the identical behavior and problems first seen in the parent-child relationship.

Thank God both Romeo and Juliet killed themselves before we were able to chart their marriage any farther into the future when it most certainly would have descended into scenarios like this:

(*Romeo enters parlor*)

"Juliet! Juliet! My Light! I'm home! Juliet? Oh, I forgot to tell you that I ate that chocolate Easter bunny that you were . . . Juliet? Juliet? Oh no. Honey. Not dead again. Don't tell me you're dead again. Please don't be playing dead again. You were just dead on Monday. I can't call 911 twice in one week. It's too embarrassing. Juliet? Juliet?"

Well, there you have this year's Valentine's Day poster couple. A thirteen-year-old girl who likes to pretend to be dead married to a teenage murderer who has no trouble falling in love with two different girls on the same Sunday night.

Which leaves us with this slightly comforting fact:

There is no reason to lament today's lack of viable romantic models. Things are no worse now than they ever were. The only difference is that back then no one watched Oprah or read psychology books. So they didn't mind calling deranged neurotic behavior "the greatest love story ever told."

Happy Valentine's Day.

Devote a day to a real, old-fashioned spring cleaning.

• • •

ANATOMY OF A MESS

One crucial key to peace of mind is the feeling that you are the master of your immediate environment. It comes in the calm that washes over you as you look around your home and breathe a gentle sigh of relief that everything is neat and clean and under control. The reason I rarely, if ever, experience anything remotely like peace of mind is that at any given moment my immediate environment reminds me of a truck without brakes headed down a steep hill toward a brick wall, growing closer and closer to complete disaster with each passing second.

For most of my life I have been at war with someone about something related to cleaning. My mother, like many women of her generation, cleaned constantly and compulsively. She believed that if you ever actually *saw* dirt, you had let things go too far. She ironed sheets and underwear. She worried about the underside of faucets. I remember with clarity the genuine confusion in my mind when she would send me into the living room to clean it up. I would look around at what appeared to me to be a perfectly clean room, searching desperately for visual clues about what exactly I was expected to do. Receiving none, I'd plump a few pillows, maybe move a few pieces of furniture just slightly to the left, or moisten a couple of surfaces and then dry them off again. I'd run the vacuum cleaner randomly over recently vacuumed rugs. To me it was a conundrum equal to the one about the falling tree in the forest that either does or does not make a sound. If your task is to clean a completely clean room, how do you know when you are finished? If I actually *asked* these questions my mother would get exasperated and angry. "You mean to tell me," she'd say, "that you have lived here all these years and still don't know the answer to that without having to ask me?"

The *good* news for me is that according to *The New York Times*, immaculate, ceaseless, compulsive housekeeping appears to be on the wane. The *bad* news for me is that I am still having trouble finding a comfortable level of cleanliness that I can maintain and also have any sort of a life.

Over the years I have taken various approaches to cleaning depending on the specifics of my living situation. When I lived with men, they, like my mom—thanks to that old favorite "repetition compulsion"—usually had fairly stringent if sometimes mysterious cleaning demands. Not that they themselves were planning to act on them. I remember a typical but particularly annoying example of this which was centered around the complaint that there were "fingerprints on the light switches." Until that moment, it had never occurred to me to do any light switch maintenance at all, let alone bathe them and wax them and buff them to a high-gloss shine. Of course, the offended guy in question wasn't doing this either. He was far too busy, much too tired. He had only just enough energy to point the problem out to me and scold me like a puppy he couldn't manage to get paper trained, but sadly not enough to actually *locate* some kind of damp cloth and remove those horrifying fingerprints himself. The last remark we exchanged on the topic, before the ground skirmishes broke out, was, I believe, when I asked him whether or not he was in fact licensed to operate a sponge in that state. The way it seemed to work with these guys was that if *they* left something out it was to be left alone. But if *I* left something out it was "*a horrible mess.*"

Later, when I was living by myself, a revolutionary notion occurred to me: that cleaning could be an act *inspired by the presence of dirt!* In fact, the existence of any visible clean areas quickly became evidence that I still had plenty of lead time. And, of course, the more arduous my schedule the less likely I was to get around to cleaning before I really had to. I think this was when I realized I was still in a cleaning war with someone—and that someone was now me. Because I began to grow ever more nervous about how things around me could barrel out of control, right before my eyes, without ever *seeing* it happen.

One minute everything would seem to be fine. Floors pretty clean. Surfaces pretty empty. So I'd lie down to take a nap. And by the time I awoke the place would look like the smoking ruins of a village under siege somewhere in the mountains behind Sarajevo. There would be wreckage. There would be carnage. There would be howling winds and sniper fire. And

I would be at a real loss even to explain how it happened. All I could do was sit, shivering under a blanket in the dark, sobbing gently into the night.

For a while I hired a Guatemalan woman to do some basic cleaning for me—an act that, as it turned out, filled me with tremendous guilt. I came to see her as a living symbol of my inadequacies. That she couldn't speak any English made me nervous, maybe because I couldn't comfort her about the two small children she had left behind motherless and poverty-stricken, living in a crumbling violent dictatorship, so that she would be able to help *me,* for low wages, keep my refrigerator free from gooey munge. To say nothing of what her presence in my home was doing to my chances of *ever* becoming attorney general.

A few weeks after her departure, it occurred to me that perhaps the solution was to analyze the situation scientifically. If I could logically, clinically, put my finger on how my house was able to go from "pretty clean" to "hazardous dump site" in a few short seconds, maybe I could learn to catch that snowball before it rolled all the way to hell. So I began to monitor my every move with extreme precision. What follows are the transcriptions of my study.

How a Mess Is Born—The Shocking Truth

8:00 A.M. The house is completely clean. I spent the day yesterday doing my best and today it's a delight to wake up here. Feeling relaxed and peaceful, I sit down with my muffin and coffee to read the morning paper. Whoops. A couple of crumbs of muffin have escaped my mouth and hit the floor. I make a note to attend to them as soon as breakfast is finished.

Uh-oh. What is all that noise? Why is my giant herd of dogs whirling like a hair tornado to the front door, smashing their noses and tongues against the glass? (Make a note: redo front door glass.) Oh, It's just the mailman. (Make a note to run the vacuum in the entry hall—it already looks like the inside of a dog-hair sweater.)

Might as well check the mail. Dumb coupons. Junk mail. A big manila envelope from my accountant. Damn. There's the phone. I'll just put the mail down here and be right back in a minute.

9:08 A.M. Now where was I again? I was going to sweep up those . . . *Oh my God! The humanity!* Let me describe the scene in front of me. It looks as if a hurricane has blown through. There are open vats of industrial waste. Windows are broken. The kitchen is full of swamp water. The living room is a smoldering ruin. Buzzards are circling overhead. Babies and small children are crying. And I don't even *have* any kids!!! *Dear God! Only minutes ago this place was a safe haven and now this!!*

What Have We Learned?

As I carefully examine this horrifying sequence of events I have been able to conclude only one thing: that the formation of a disastrous mess is somehow inextricably linked to *the arrival of mail*. Perhaps there is something inherently evil in the electromagnetic particles of everything that comes in contact with the U.S. Postal Service, also explaining the reason so many postal workers go berserk and shoot their supervisors and fellow employees. Yes, this is only a theory. But as of now science can offer none better. So, until more is known, my best suggestion is this: Rent yourself a room to live in at a nearby motel and arrange to have your mail delivered there. Visit yourself, at your home, only for short periods of time when absolutely necessary. When you do, bring a broom and some Lysol. And keep your fingers crossed.

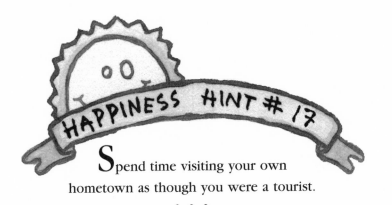

Spend time visiting your own
hometown as though you were a tourist.

• • •

MERRILL MARKOE'S GUIDE TO
HOLLYWOOD BOULEVARD

Eventually, everyone who lives in Los Angeles has to answer
questions from out-of-town visitors. The answer to the first
question is obvious: "I've heard that for years, but how can it
be true? The guy had a wife and kids!" But when they ask the
second question, which is generally about what to do the day
after they've been to Disneyland and Universal Studios, the
idea of "seeing Hollywood" inevitably arises. I realized recently that I no longer had any idea what, if anything, there is
to see or do on the Hollywood Boulevard Walk of Fame. And
so, after I successfully wrestled my own enormous resistance
to the area back to the mat, I went to no small amount of trouble to create:

The Markoe Walking Tour
of Hollywood Boulevard

1. Park your car somewhere near the **Chinese Theater,** taking care to observe the bountiful harvest of pear-shaped people ripening the area year-round. Looking skyward, stop to enjoy the newest version of the Newport billboard. In this one, the "alive with pleasure" couple seems to be out of control on a riding mower—surely one of their best dates ever! Now *cross the street. . . .*

2. Sooner or later you will feel compelled to go into one of the many nearly identical "gift" stores, so I say get it over with right away. And of course, when I say "gift," I am using the broadest possible definition. Who exactly do you know who would enjoy this assortment of T-shirts, ceramic cups, plaques, and posters all bearing a likeness of James Dean or Marilyn Monroe? So stop in at **Rocket Hollywood,** where in addition to the previously described items you can also purchase not just one but *two* varieties of rubber vomit! Choose between a sort of mixed grill (which claims to be "great fun at home, parties and the office") and a kind of ground beef and hominy sauté (which offers fun at all of the aforementioned venues plus "auto" and "patios").

3. **The Guinness World of Records Museum,** just adjacent to **Arnold Schwarzenegger.** It's $7.50 to get in (or for $12, you can save three dollars overall by also buying a ticket to the Hollywood Wax Museum across the street). And what a museum it is! A bit smaller than the Louvre, but where else can you find a statue of Elvis that is so unrecognizable that you have to read the label to know who it is? Other favorite exhibits are:

• St. Simeon the Younger (A.D. 521–597), *the man who sat on a column for forty-five years!* I bet not one person since has even *tried* to do forty-five years.

• The hologram of Michael Hebranko losing 688 pounds in two years and then ballooning back up again, right before our eyes—just one of the many tributes to gluttony throughout the museum, which range from the spectacular (a videotape of someone eating 144 prunes in 35 seconds) to the mundane (a videotape of someone eating 250 oysters in two minutes, 52 seconds). Come on! I myself can eat 300 oysters in two minutes flat, just one of the many reasons I am year in and year out one of the most sought-after dining companions in the city of Los Angeles.

4. Now it's back to the Walk of Fame where you'll soon come across the **Crosby, Still and Nash** star, which turns out to be the gateway to the **Heavy Metal Accessories District.** Here you have a chance to review every variation on studded leather emblazoned with skulls currently being manufactured. The price is right for bondage anklets studded with bullets, so load up! They make excellent stocking stuffers! Or head on down to **Rhonda Fleming** and a store that offers some of the most imaginative spelling in town (I was particularly impressed by "neckless"). Now it's time to *skedaddle on over to* **Gordon Jenkins** for a real tour highlight . . .

5. **The Outfitters Wig Shop Window.** The female wig heads are merely indescribable, but the males! How about that young Martin Mull look-alike, resplendent in what appears to

be white head bandages yet still very nicely coiffed . . . as though he were preparing to enjoy a lovely evening out not long after serious brain surgery. Or my personal favorite, the anonymous white guy with the Afro and sunglasses who seems to be thinking he's looking pretty damn jaunty in spite of his prominent cold sore. *And so, move on to . . .*

6. **Frederick's of Hollywood.** As you enter, pause to notice the male mannequin in the black shorty silk robe and matching boxer shorts who sports a haughty expression that seems to scream. "Please! Someone! Just kill me!" Inside, in addition to the oft-discussed behemoth assortment of underwear permutations, stop in and visit **The Lingerie Museum.** There, amid tableaux detailing the invention of such cultural marvels as the underwire bra (and photos of Mr. Frederick with such unlikely soulmates as Woody Allen and Tom Waits), pause to consider these words from Mr. Frederick: "Bare your nipples but be smart and put your *breasts on a shelf.*" I'm not sure what that means, but I have a feeling that it's as true today as the day it was written.

7. Now a quick jog up to **Olga Petrova** and **Hollywood's Largest Toy Shop,** where you'll find excellent buys on "prosthetic forearm wounds" and "burn sears." (Talk about birthday gifts!) Now, *sprint across the street without getting hit by a car to . . .*

8. **Another wig shop window,** this one fittingly adjacent to **Martha Raye,** where you can view a few vivid examples of how Meg Ryan can be expected to look several years after she has been embalmed.

9. It's at this point in the tour when, seeing yet another photo of the scowling James Dean peering out at me from a store window, I begin to think to myself, "If this guy wasn't already dead, I might have to strangle him myself." This is a little clue that the charm of Hollywood Boulevard is beginning to wear thin. And so I break out in full *run to my car.* . . . But wait!

10. There's the **Wax Museum!** My God! I was stupid enough to have bought that discount ticket back across the street! Now I pretty much *have* to at least walk in the damn place! The Wax Museum is a great place to bring your high-roller gambler friends because you are *guaranteed* to win a bundle of money if you bet them that they cannot identify the celebrity replicas without looking at the name labels. Thanks presumably to the same people who made the unrecognizable Elvis back at the Guinness Museum, you are safe wagering any amount of money that your pals will not be able to identify Bob Hope, Kelly McGillis, Tom Cruise, Robert Redford, Jack Nicholson, Tom Hanks, Kevin Costner . . . even Marilyn Monroe! Roy Rogers looks hydrocephalic. *Will* Rogers appears to be suffering from dementia praecox. Lucia Mendez is an amazingly accurate likeness. But since no one I speak to has any idea who she is, she poses an entirely different problem.

11. Okay, now you can *leave.* The quicker the better. The good news is that when your friends ask you what you did today, you can tell them you went to *three different museums!* And as you drive home safely in your own little car, smile quietly to yourself and remember that there is no law that says you ever have to go *back* to the Walk of Fame again.

Start to write your own book
or short story.

• • •

WOMEN WHO
HONK WITH THE GEESE

Much has been said of the women who run with the wolves! The ones who toss their manes of raven or flaxen hair and howl to the moon in an anguished cry at the loss of their wildish natures. I do not know these women or the wolves with whom they go running. For I wish to speak now of the women who move to the call of a different mythological archetype. These are the women who make dozens of trips to the refrigerator that they already know is empty, each time hoping that some new, heretofore unobserved food item has magically appeared without them having to get dressed and go out to the store. These are the women that do not realize that the impassioned speech they have been delivering is being undercut by the fact that they have bread crumbs in their eyebrows. I speak now of the women who honk with the geese.

Those of us who hear the calling of the goose woman know she is beside us when we are trying to sound sexy on the portable phone and suddenly it begins to make noises as though we are in a beehive at the bottom of the sea. There she is at our aerobics class as we do our hip hop moves, feeling in our hearts that we could possibly get work as a fly girl because we have some real natural dance ability, unlike that poor person over there in the corner who looks like Baby Huey in a leotard. And then we realize we are looking into a mirror and that Baby Huey is *us*. When a passionate kiss is interrupted by noisy stomach rumbles, we feel the spirit of the goose woman. When we dine at a lovely restaurant and an entire wonton slides off our spoon and onto our lap, we can hear her honking and we know we have returned to our gooselike ways.

Fable of the Goose Woman

Once long ago in a land that was east of the sun and west of the moon—well actually it was northwest, just where the I-405 meets Route 10—there was a handsome prince who had great material wealth, but his heart was very lonely and sad. He was thirty and seven years old and longed for the love of a woman who would make his soul sing.

Late one afternoon he was doing the medieval equivalent of speed walking through the meadow near his castle when he came to a clearing where a group of women were dancing in the fading afternoon light. He hid himself behind a pine bough to watch in secret and quickly fell under the spell of Jennifer, the fairest among them. She could do "Running Man" like Bobby Brown. Each afternoon at the same time he returned to the clearing in the meadow to watch and finally after four days and three he realized that his love had grown so strong that his heart cried out to meet her. So he stepped forward to offer her flowers and frankincense and other medieval gift items as a gesture of his good will and noble intentions. At first she was frightened. Her girlfriends advised her to be wary but his earnest pleas for her company began to take effect and she agreed to meet him alone in the evening, to share a meal.

Almost from the moment their evening together began Jennifer realized there was magic between them. The lonely prince provided candlelight and rare delicacies to eat. He serenaded her sweetly on the lute. And even though Jennifer had never really been one for lute music she realized she was surrendering her heart against her own best instincts. By the evening's end, the prince confessed how much he had enjoyed her company. He was tired of being all alone. And when he knelt to kiss her it was a kiss both gentle and passionate. It made her head feel like it was about to spin off her torso, like the medieval equivalent of the little possessed girl in *The Exorcist*.

And so she was so saddened to say goodbye she almost shed a tear. But the lonely prince promised that they would speak the very next night. They would arrange another rendezvous that would bring them together again.

For four nights and three Jennifer sat awaiting some word from the lonely prince. As her anxiety began to grow she called all the members of her late afternoon dance group together and asked them what they thought she should do. "Well," said the smartest among them, "perhaps the reason you have not heard from him is that he has fallen ill." Jennifer gasped because this had never occurred to her. So she arranged to have a note of inquiry delivered.

Now Jennifer waited for three more nights and on the fourth when she heard nothing still she called all the late afternoon dancing girls together again to seek further advice.

"Well, you're beautiful, you're independent, you're smart, you're a good dancer . . . maybe he's intimidated by you," they suggested. "Why don't *you* ask *him* out this time?"

So Jennifer saddled up a steed and rode to the castle. When she informed the guards that she was here to see the prince, she was a little surprised they had no idea who she was.

When she finally was able to confront him face-to-face, she could sense immediately that something was different even though he *said* it was nice to see her, and apologized for not calling because he claimed he had been very busy. Nevertheless, he *promised* he would check the royal day planner and call her as soon as his schedule returned to normal.

Jennifer never heard from the lonely prince again. Within four days and twenty she had gained eleven pounds. She never figured out what happened exactly. Later, one of the women in her dance group said she heard he had gotten back together with an old girlfriend. Another one said she heard he might be gay.

And sometimes when the moon is full, and you look to the horizon, they say you can see Jennifer, eating and honking and running in circles.

Today when we hear the honking of the geese in the distant skies we think of the story of Jennifer and the lonely prince. And we get up to see if anything new has appeared by magic in the refrigerator. And we go to the phone and call up the answering machine of someone we used to know and when he picks up and says hello, we hang up. And then we go to the store and buy old cupcakes and eat them in front of the television. But we can barely hear what the generic-looking white men in suits are saying because the honking of the goose woman is drowning them out.

Redecorate your home to
really please yourself.

• • •

HOUSE AND KARMA

I have always had interior decorating problems. I'm not as
bad as one guy I met who not only had not a stick of furniture,
but also hung all his suits in the bathroom on the shower cur-
tain. On the other hand, I'm not like various friends of mine
who spend their free time looking at sconces and those dec-
orative knobs that you can add to the top of a lamp shade. I'm
not even sure what sconces are. Perhaps this is one of the reasons why when my friend Robin received a flyer from someone selling her services as a "psychic interior decorator," she
immediately turned it over to me.

After actors, I think psychics are probably the richest and
most diverse category of L.A. hyphenates. My smart, successful friend Carol once consulted a psychic-nutritionist, a man
who determined her nutritional deficiencies by passing what

she describes as a "clicker, kind of like a hole puncher" up and down her spinal cord. She thinks *perhaps* his services helped a little, but she does recall her reason for terminating them. It was the day he determined that she had an allergy to formaldehyde and proposed that she combat it by bringing all of her leather belongings—belts, shoes, purses, and, of course, wallets—into his office so he could detoxify them by "clicking" over them. Good or bad, this is the kind of personal service that she probably could not have gotten if she lived somewhere else.

Which brings me back to the psychic interior decorator. My friend Robin had no idea how she had come to be the target of this rather specific mass mailing. "Psychic attunement blended with practical interior design creates magic in your home" is what the flyer said. "Rediscover your LIFE THEME collections buried deep within your own friendly clutter. . . . Unlock and guide the flow of energy through your home." "Someone handed me a list and said, 'These people need you,' " the sender explained to me when I finally met her. The author was Sandra Be-Taylor, "highly creative psychic and interior designer."

Her pamphlet filled me with a longing to hear her find a "life theme" from within my "friendly clutter." There are friendly clutters and then there's *my* friendly clutter. I save crap. I can't control it. I don't even try. I have forty-four snow shakers from airports around the world, not because I think they're so beautiful but because after I had three I felt I should go the distance, since they're usually under five bucks a pop. I save a lot of things because I find them funny. That's the only explanation I can give for my growing cereals-named-after-movies collection. (I just bought the Prince of Thieves. I can hardly wait for The Prince of Tides.) I don't understand what these cereals *are*—recipes from the production staff? But I do feel it is incumbent upon me to own them all in case I am called upon to contribute to a time capsule at the millennium.

I tried to imagine what Sandra Be would say about all this stuff. I thought perhaps she would relate the snow shakers to Atlantis in winter. I couldn't even fantasize what she'd make of the cereals. But I did feel certain this would be the greatest challenge of her young career.

When I spoke to her on the phone I had a psychic premonition of my own about what she would look like. A picture of an extremely well-groomed, tight-lipped black woman in her thirties, à la Anita Hill, came to me as if in a vision. When she greeted me at her door, and turned out to be an effervescent, petite white woman in her thirties with long red curly hair, dressed in a sweatshirt and black tights, I was pretty impressed at how close I'd gotten. I *knew* she was in her thirties!

"I feel like everything I've ever done in my life has led up to doing psychic interiors," she told me. "You think it's odd. I think it's practical. It's a perfect combination."

"You have a book coming out," she said a couple of minutes later. This was true. "You must take responsibility for getting yourself on the talk shows," she went on. "I'm doing everything in my power to keep from reading you."

Before she became a hyphenate, she had been a jewelry designer, regular plain old psychic and a straight interior decorator. "But I couldn't really do it," she explained, "because the straight interior designer credo is 'get rid of everything,' since the more your client buys, the more money you make. So to be a straight interior decorator is to be slightly inauthentic to your client."

As she described her work, some of her tales of interior decorating challenges were fairly standard stuff involving chaotic messes created by men too busy to know which room they were supposed to sleep in. "But I get to the bedroom of this one place," she tells me, giving me an example of her unique hyphenate skills in action, "and it was like somebody slapped me. I went through the door and aah! It threw me up against the wall. The previous occupant had been so unhappy in that bedroom that they cried themselves to sleep from loneliness. So when I went in there I started to cry. I had to do a major cleansing ritual in that room."

After we agreed she'd come to my house, I thought to myself that perhaps she'd better wear a crash helmet because of all the sliding glass doors. "It's possible to heal and transform your environment and make yourself feel great," she told me. "I could go into your house and in a second pull out what's important to you." I was psyched. I wanted to see her do it.

"When I enter this house," she said, coming through my front door and heading straight past my dining room and into my den, "I get that your soul is here. This is your heartbeat." She stopped right in front of the shelves full of my "collections." "This is a power spot in your house," she said, picking up my framed and autographed photo of Captain Kangaroo. "This epitomizes who you are." "Yeah, but what do you think of how much crap I have?" I asked her. "I see warmth," she said to me. "I see history. There's a sacred beauty here."

I think this was the moment when she won my heart. "God bless you," I said to her. "You're officially the first person to relate to my crap as beautiful." "But *you're* the person this house is *for*," she replied, laughing at how bewildered I looked. "We need to reempower your house. I get the feeling of non-inhabitedness.

"This room feels like an orphan," she said of the living room, which I'd been keeping clutter-free in the name of . . . well, I don't know in the name of what. I felt I shouldn't degrade it with my stuff, and as a result I seldom went in there. "What I want to give you is a sense of being warm and safe and nurtured in your own home," she said as she pulled stuff off the shelves in the den and put it all over the formerly empty living room.

And so it came to pass that a psychic interior decorator gave me permission to put my own stuff in my own living room. You'd think this would have occurred to me on my own, but I have no evidence it would have. And now because of a psychic interior decorator I like to hang out in there for the first time.

Truly a service that would never have been available to me had I not lived in Los Angeles, of this I feel certain.

Visualize a future in which
the world will be a better place.

• • •

MANNERS FOR THE

MILLENNIUM

The next century will be a time of many informational break-
throughs. Most notably, the battle between the sexes will take
on a new complexion because it will be scientifically docu-
mented that men and women are completely different species
(not unlike, say, hyenas and pumas, although there will be a
lot of heated arguments about who gets to be the pumas).

Once everyone accepts that we're speaking different lan-
guages, a computer system will be developed that allows instantaneous intersexual communication to occur. For the first
time, certain simple but formerly bewildering transactions will
become clear. At the end of an evening out, when the single
man of the future says to his date, "I had a nice time. I'll call
you" (I predict that men will still be using this line), the
woman to whom he is speaking will immediately hear in her

headset: "What he means is that while he thinks you are attractive, he's concerned that you already have expectations of him that he will never be able to meet. He's associating you with his needy, castrating mother because she had the same hair color as yours."

By this time, sex and dating will be so dangerous (owing to numerous rampant communicable diseases and personality disorders) that they will be attempted only by the kind of thrill seekers who now do things like bungee jumping, sky surfing, and eating at Denny's. By the year 2020, in fact, "casual dating" will be a popular arena sport. People too terrified to pursue something so hazardous themselves will witness actual live human beings who, for big money stakes, will eat dinner with and then perhaps (if dinner goes well) become intimate with people they are attracted to but basically know nothing about.

Because the average person will be far too cautious to risk even a single totally worthless encounter, we will see the transformation of the medical clinic into a kind of after-hours club where nervous but lonely people will be able to undergo a battery of health tests and, while awaiting the results, stop by the bar to enjoy a trendy snack with others who may have the same ailment. (I predict that honey-roasted songbirds will be the snack of choice by then because they will turn out to be the last remaining edible creature that is domestically plentiful, low in fat, and still has not been made into a trendy snack item.)

All of this escalating terror will, oddly, increase the number of marriages taking place, even though we will see the divorce rate rise from one in two marriages to two in two. These alarming statistics will cause the birth of a new nuptial tradition. Savvy couples will create the most intimate bond two people can share by agreeing to get married and divorced simultaneously. At that point, they will possess so much file data about each other that they will negotiate in advance the terms of every day they plan to spend together, deciding what annoying habits they are willing to tolerate and, more important, what personal details each one will permit the other to use either in court or in the eventual tell-all book. "Looking at me cross-eyed" could emerge as the most common charge of misconduct in the personal nuisance suits that will clog the legal system.

Playing right into that will be the amount of specific evidence people will have accumulated about each other as "compulsive video documentation" becomes the most common new addiction. By the year 2010, TV networks will decide to give all video-equipment owners a shot at their own show as long as they promise to supply footage that is extremely disturbing. Recorded evidence of violence and malicious mayhem will draw such astronomical sums that criminals contemplating an illegal activity will consult with movie developers during the important planning stages of the crime. They will thus make sure that the approach they are taking with regard to plot and details is the one that will have the best eventual effect on sales figures and marketing potential.

This blurring of the line between life and entertainment will culminate in a scandal when a giant underground facility is discovered in the Midwest that is being used as a breeding lab by desperate talk-show producers who have been completely out of new guests since the mid-1990s. It will be discovered that the producers have been assembling affable humanoids from the fat, tissue, bone, and spare parts of celebrities who have undergone a lot of plastic surgery, training the "guests" to cultivate zany or inappropriate hobbies and schooling them in how to tell ten different fifteen-minute anecdotes about themselves. This will constitute their entire life-span, after which they will be melted down and reworked for an additional booking.

Yes, it's going to be a bold new world, full of brand new dysfunctions, addictions, and disorders: a million new things to worry about! But that's progress.

Attend a local production
of a play or musical.

• • •

Puzzled People
Cannot Laugh

I guess I've always been kind of a media bandwagon party pooper. Even during my formative years (those cavity-prone ages of six through twelve), as soon as I would sense any real show of group spirit forming, I would begin to check the room for emergency exits.

Nowadays I continue right along with this proud tradition by sitting mute at sing-alongs and remaining planted during the wave at ball games. In fact, it's all I can do to bring myself to attend a movie that has proven to be a big box-office hit. And I might as well add that this spoilsport attitude goes double for anything offering mandatory nostalgia. I don't find the fifties adorable. And as the effort goes on to enshrine the sixties and seventies in diners and coffeehouses, I am fully prepared to loathe those too.

I reveal all this by way of an explanation before I tell you the awful truth: *The Real Live Brady Bunch* at the Westwood Playhouse came very close to making me lose the will to live. And it's not because this new, ironically acted stage version of classic television crap didn't make me laugh. It's pretty funny.

No, it wasn't the performance of *The Real Live Brady Bunch* that bummed me out so bad. It was, for lack of a better way to explain it, the Zen reality of the whole experience . . . beginning with the guy who sat down next to the friend I brought with me and tried to hit on her by displaying his truly encyclopedic knowledge of "Brady Bunch" trivia. Then there were the people dancing up and down the aisles to the tape of carefully chosen lame seventies' songs (like "Boogie Oogie Oogie" and "Billy, Don't Be a Hero"), acting like they were part of a pretty special club: people who remember lots of lame things about the seventies. Maybe this was depressing to me because it proved our culture has gotten so hollow that even the wimpiest, weirdest shared memory of just a few years ago has become a cause for nostalgic bonding.

Which brings us to the strange and terrifying transformation of the creator-producer of "The Brady Bunch" and "Gilligan's Island," Sherwood Schwartz, from cornball bad-television perpetrator to cutting-edge hip comedy guru. It's a story that I think speaks to the heart of my problem with the whole deal.

When I met Sherwood Schwartz about a year and a half ago, I was very taken by what a sweet guy he was. This was despite the fact that his musical oeuvre (the theme songs he cowrote for "The Brady Bunch" and "Gilligan's Island") has been responsible for grievous bodily injuries to me, as I have been forced over the years to hurl myself with a violence that frightens me over and under pieces of furniture, searching hysterically for access to the piece of equipment that will allow me to turn off the volume on the television before I have to hear the completion of the phrase that begins "Here's the story of a lovely lady. . . ." Only the theme to "Three's Company" (featuring the uniquely odious lyric "There's a lovable space that needs your face . . . three's company too") has been responsible for more of my serious sprains, bruises and puncture wounds. (When I asked Schwartz why he felt the need to have the entire premise of "The Brady Bunch" set forth musically at the start of every episode, he explained, "Puzzled people cannot laugh.")

At the time, it was clear that in addition to amazing financial wealth (I'm just guessing here), Schwartz's extremely well known cultural contributions had brought him some light-hearted contempt. "My wife and I were in Dana Point at this little restaurant on the water," he recalled for me, "and as we sat down I said, 'What a lovely place, what a lovely place . . .' I knew it was a double line from a song, but I couldn't think what one. So I asked this young waitress, 'Do you know where it comes from?' and she said, 'Yes. The Eagles. "Hotel California." ' A few minutes later I said, 'Maybe you can help me out again. There's another line that I can't remember where it comes from. A *three-hour tour, a three-hour tour . . .*' and she said, 'What's the matter with you? I'm not going to even dignify that with a reply. Why are you even asking me that?' and I said, 'Because I wrote it,' and she said, 'Sure you did,' and went away and almost refused to serve us."

Yet even then, he had begun to experience a taste of what was to come. "I just got back from Evansville," he told me, referring to the university there, "and every place I went all the kids in the class got up to sing the song." And so it came to pass that Sherwood Schwartz was transformed into a man of comedic hipness without having to rethink or rewrite a single sentence.

Underlying this seemingly inexplicable phenomenon is the horrible truth that there is a dangerous chasm at the center of the safe little dumb spot we laughingly refer to as our culture. All that binds us is shared dopey media experiences. Awful, stupid stuff to which we've all been subjected. And I guess that's why *The Real Live Brady Bunch* bummed me out so bad. I mean, I feel optimistic and happy every time I hear a new record that I like. Or a movie sneaks through that actually has some thought behind it. Or someone writes something that is fun to read. But here in the theater were all these theoretically smart, funny people, and after all was said and done . . . it was still "The Brady Bunch." *Again!*

Maybe I'm taking this too hard. Perhaps I'm dyspeptic. Excuse me while I go take a hot bath.

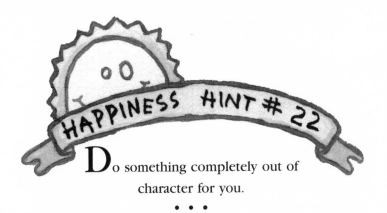

Do something completely out of
character for you.

• • •

HOW TO PLEASE A MAN EVERY TIME AND HAVE HIM OKAY MAYBE NOT BEG FOR MORE BUT AT LEAST NOT DEMAND A WHOLE LOT LESS

Through my very special home-brewed blend of insecurity,
moon blindness and some sort of nonspecific mineral defi-
ciency, I have spent much of my life totally unable to accu-
rately read the sexual signals sent me by the opposite sex.
So truly terrible am I at this, I have actually had men I invited
into my home (after a pleasant evening out together) hanging
around until three or four in the morning and still not been
able to tell if it was safe to interpret their behavior as evidence
of sexual interest. Perhaps, I would reason to myself, they are

grateful to have found shelter and are harboring the delusion that if they hang in a while longer they might eventually receive some hot soup.

It always seemed to me that to presume anything more was to open myself up to the risk of a painful rejection. And thus, the only clue that such a date was actually interested in a physical encounter of any kind came after the man in question had passed out cold, having endured all he could stand of hours on end of my fascinating childhood reminiscences. Any subsequent attempts I might make to try to revive him would amount to the only contact that would ever take place.

Of course, that was the *old* me. Now I know better. Not because I have become more astute but because over the years I have had it repeatedly explained to me by numerous men of reasonable intelligence that the adult human male does *not* hang around endlessly in a place he does not want to be unless he has a sexual motive. I have been bluntly advised that it would be safe for me to go ahead and presume that any man exhibiting a willingness to listen to even *one* consecutive hour of my fascinating childhood stories is interested in more than just another hour of my fascinating childhood stories.

Okay. That understood, I have moved forward and developed a slick method of seductive maneuvering that can carry a person forward from that point.

MERRILL'S FIVE STEPS TO A SEXUAL SEDUCTION

1. Offer him something to drink. It is, of course, incredibly important to remember to *have something drinkable somewhere on the premises.* How many were the times when I have made this offer only to discover, to my embarrassment, that the only remotely drinkable liquid in my refrigerator was a small amount of either canola oil or no-fat ranch-style dressing. And the truth is, even when served on the rocks in a lovely cut glass crystal goblet, neither one seems to get a very favorable response.

2. This accomplished, next comes the old "let me slip into something more comfortable." This step, too, is fraught with pitfalls if you, like me in most instances, make the mistake of wearing something quite comfortable in the first place. Now you are faced with the seemingly unsolvable dilemma of try-ing to find something *more* comfortable than the jeans and sweater you already have on. Forget about anything you may have purchased from the Victoria's Secret catalog. That stuff is all much less comfortable. Which is why you must com-mit to memory this critical dating rule: Always wear some-thing *uncomfortable* out on a date. Only then can you really provide yourself with the fullest range of eventual changing options.

3. Now sit down with your potential beloved on a piece of furniture large enough for two and attempt to initiate a seduc-tive vibe through eye contact. The best way to kick this off is to encourage him to talk about something *he* finds fasci-nating—like why Ferraris are cooler than Porsches. In many cases this will amount to something you can barely pay atten-tion to, but do not worry about that because this type of man tends to feel that the act of hearing himself talk about some-thing of interest only to him in fact constitutes having a con-versation. The rest of the good news is that later, when he

thinks back on how the evening went, he will recall that *you* were a really good conversationalist!

4. Meanwhile, use this important down time to begin reciting silently that most powerful mantra of seduction—the one that is virtually guaranteed to draw the attractive man of your dreams to you like malaria to a mosquito. Say it with me now: *"Come here. Go away. Come here. Go away. I love you. I really don't want you. Come here. Go away. Come here. Go away."* For maximum effectiveness we must now borrow a page from that most successful group of seducers—the serial killers. Deranged? Nuts? Yes, absolutely, but never without willing sexual partners or a date on a Saturday night. Why? Well, perhaps it is that magnetic facial expression which seems to combine a radiant vulnerable loving smile with the detached gaze of a slaughterhouse foreman or a movie star on his way into a drug rehab program. *Why* this works is not important. It works, that's all we know. (In fact, we're all better off not knowing why it works, aren't we?)

5. How long should you keep this up? Well, if after a good hour nothing much seems to be happening, consult your watch and move on to the final powerful step. Wait for the first conversational lull and then jump in with both feet and begin to dominate with stories from your childhood. If, after twenty-five minutes, you find your date is still both present *and* feigning interest, assume he has the hots for you. Go ahead and make your move.

Postscript

Because not every completed seduction attempt leads to anything particularly pleasing I feel compelled to answer the following common question before it has even been asked: QUESTION: How many times should you allow a guy to slam your head into the wall behind your bed before you officially declare it "bad sex" and attempt to abort the proceedings? ANSWER: Two. The first time, it is still possible that it was only an accident.

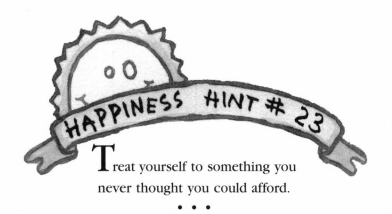

Treat yourself to something you
never thought you could afford.

• • •

A Tenacious Grasp
of the Obvious

As a kind of a pointless brain teaser, I sometimes used to ponder during televised sportscasts what the irritating media equivalent of a televised sportscast for the non–sports fan might
be . . . just in case I ever got a chance to inflict some sort of
separate but equal revenge on an obsessed sports fanatic as
retribution for the endless hours of sports broadcasts I have
been made to endure over the years. What, if anything, I
would ask myself, could possibly grate on their nerves the
way the sound of droning play-by-play announcers inter-
mixed with ambient crowd noises seems to grate on mine?
And nothing seemed remotely hellish enough. Not the
Weather Channel, not even Barney the Dinosaur . . . Until that
sunny afternoon when I first encountered a home shopping
show.

I immediately realized I had found the excruciating revenge I was seeking. Except for one fatal drawback. *I* wouldn't be able both to inflict it and stick around to revel in the results the way the sports fan can. Because home shopping is the only thing I have ever seen on TV that makes speed boat racing and afternoon golf seem not just watchable, but riveting and exciting by comparison.

Recently I heard fashion mogul Diane Von Furstenberg and media mogul Barry Diller conjecturing that they really couldn't visualize the TV owner who would not eventually be an eager home shopping participant. I suppose I ought to send them each my photo. I keep hearing that home shopping shows are popular, even addictive, but I don't understand how anyone can bear them. Starting with the stunning fact that they have finally succeeded in developing a category of television performer even more vile, superficial, and witless than the game-show host and the wacky weatherman combined.

I have heard it said more than once that these "shopping hosts" are like "family" to their regular viewers. And I can understand that because in the real world the only circumstances under which I would tolerate this level of tedious empty-headed babbling are the occasions on which I have been trapped by tradition and politeness at various family functions.

There is a simple mathematical theorem that clearly explains my discomfort. A: the fact that I am someone who does not like to be talked to as though I were an idiot PLUS B: the fact that I also do not like to hear the opinion of salespeople when I am contemplating a purchase at a store PLUS C: the fact that these hosts seem to have been hired primarily for their ability to go on endlessly stating and restating the obvious in thousands of different ways until the product is all sold out EQUALS D: a video presentation as close to my own personal definition of "truly irritating" as I am anxious to get.

A portrait of one of these "hosts" written up in a Home Shopping Network publication called *The Bargaineer* listed among his qualifications "doing commercials for Toyota and Neutrogena Soap." "He thinks the best thing about the job," the article went on to say, "is the people calling in to talk. 'They're the real entertainment,' he says, 'they're the real stars.' "

Which brings us to the way in which home shopping has also succeeded in lessening "the minimum definition of entertainment"—a title that previously fell somewhere in between "calling a 900 number astrology forecast line" and "trying to get rid of the Jehovah's Witnesses on your porch." Not since Chevy Chase lost his late-night talk show has such boring, pointless conversation been available to such a wide audience.

If a guidebook exists to advise the novice shopping host it must certainly contain the following conversational instructions: "No matter what a caller says to you, only one of two responses is ever necessary: 1. A gasp. 2. A laugh or chuckle."
Consider the following typical exchange from QVC:

CALLER: Hi. This is Laurie from San Rafael.

HOST: (Gasp) San Rafael! That's a great place to be from. Have you shopped with us before?

CALLER: Yes. I have a couple of your weskits and I like them very much.

HOST: (Chuckle) Oh! Those were a very good choice!

CALLER: What I enjoy so much about them is that you can go casual or you can go formal.

HOST: (Gasp) Very true! (Chuckle) Well, we're glad to have you back with us again today. (More chuckling)

Talk about real entertainment.

But conducting dozens of conversations that never rise above this level is only part of the job of the busy shopping host or hostess. The real meat of the job, so to speak, comes in endless hours of improvised sales pitches. There must have been a training seminar where they instructed these people to begin each pitch with an elaborate definition of even the commonest of products, followed by an endless listing of its possible uses, as though the whole thing were being viewed by someone completely new to our galaxy who might not have even the most rudimentary grasp of any of our concepts.

"It's a polished silver picture frame," I heard one guy begin his pitch on QVC, "great for any picture you might have. It's perfect for those wedding photos or maybe you have some photos of your recent vacation—this is ideal, or perhaps some photos of someone who just graduated—this would be wonderful. Or how about snapshots of the new grandchild? Or shots from the big office party . . . ?" He was just getting started.

"This is my first ruby ring," I heard Charlene of "Shopping with Charlene" on the Home Shopping Network say, "Deep dark *vivacious* [*sic*] rubies. And whether this is going to be your first ruby red ring or perhaps your tenth or your sixth or you're looking for something for the lady in your life or maybe adding to your collection . . ." *Help!* Somebody make these people stop before I go down there and do things I'm certain to regret!

Which brings us to the lingo. The language choices on home shopping shows are so full of newly minted terms for things of questionable pedigree that it amounts to the sales equivalent of a Napoleon complex. *Every* piece of jewelry has a glamorous-sounding official name. What looks like a diamond on HSN is called "cubic zirconium." It's known as "Diamonique" on QVC. A recent viewing of the "Discover Diamonique" show on QVC featured "simulated emeralds" ("It puts the true emerald to shame. It's such a lovely shade of dark green."), "Caribbean Ice," and "Lilac Ice, which some people call simulated tanzanite." ("It goes with everything. A gorgeous ring. Just perfect.") Other pieces were "designer inspired" and laden with "faux pearls," then "gold layered by techni-bond." And all of these expensive-sounding terms go drifting by, unremarked upon, as though they might actually mean something. Certain things also come with "a certificate of authenticity."

They are all part of a universe of theoretically prestigious references that seem to exist only within the boundaries of home shopping channels. This also includes "Capodimonte figurines" and "Kanchanaburi sapphires." ("Have you bought Kanchanaburi sapphires with us before?" asks Charlene. "Oh yes," says a caller. "I've got so many rings I don't know where to put them.")

And then there are the celebrity product lines. A few years ago the big name was Farrah Fawcett, who was hawking her "exclusive line of jewelry" based on "replicas of pieces she wore in movies" and "reproductions of jewelry given to her by Ryan O'Neal." I thought that was the most touching idea I'd ever heard of—turning the personal tokens of love you received from your boyfriend into a line of inexpensive jewelry for the mass market—but that was before I saw Joan Rivers on QVC just the other night selling her "pearl clasp expandable bracelet." "Fabulous! Fabulous! So elegant! So chic!" she said, explaining that it was a duplicate of a piece given to her by her late husband, Edgar Rosenberg, who we all know took his own life. Talk about a sentimental gesture! Talk about a fool for love! Joan was also offering "the Joan Rivers pavé crystal earrings—a gift from Robert Goulet." I guess the smart person should sign a contract with her before attending any holiday function where presents are exchanged.

I realize that millions of happy, satisfied viewers do not seem to be as repelled by this stuff as I am. Repelled nothing. The fanatical love they feel is palpable. "You know, Cathy, I heard you three years ago when you talked to a lady from Oakland during the big fire," I heard a QVC caller say, "and she said she had to get off. She was being evacuated." "Yes, I remember," said the host, Cathy. "You made the *San Francisco Chronicle*," the caller went on. "Her house burned down." "I know," said Cathy. "Some of our fabulous viewers sent me the article. She wrote us a follow-up letter and said she couldn't believe she was shopping at a time like that. She said she really is a rational woman and is getting her life back together." Then she went on to sell the caller a simulated emerald "with a touch of hugs and kisses on the side. The perfect ring."

It's pretty apparent that, with or without my approval, home shopping is on the rise. It does combine two national obsessions—the love of spending and the love of television.

But as for me, the only thing I personally stand to gain from its presence is that now there is programming I find so thoroughly irritating I may finally have found a motive for becoming a sports fan.

Throw out things that are no
longer a part of your life.

• • •

Rites of Purification, or How I Finally Threw Away the Recipe for "John Davidson's Turtle Brownies"

About once a year I feel the need to sweep through my home like a human tornado, leaving a lot of stuff thrown away in my wake. Well, maybe "human tornado" is a little strong. Maybe a human low pressure system is closer. But it's something I'm getting better at, which is lucky for me because I'm also a person who spends the other 364 days saving an assortment of things that should never have been saved.

I have different philosophies for the categories of items to be discarded. At the top of the list are the barely evaluated "items I will take with me to the grave." (Well, maybe not to the actual grave. Perhaps just to the edge of the cemetery, where my next of kin can set up card tables and have a very strange tag sale.) In this category are awards received, creative projects completed, photo albums, household appliances that still work, and anything that can even loosely be construed as an earring.

I am at my meteorological best when throwing away clothes. I actually find it to be a rite of purification. Brand-new empty space in the closet makes me feel that it would be a very smart move to go out and buy some new clothes right away. Why am I so comfortable with this? Because I have a time-tested theory that has served me well for over a decade. Here it is: If you don't wear something for two years, not only will you probably never wear it again, but you won't even miss it when it's gone. Remember, even if that style comes back again, you are going to want the new version.

Unfortunately, this edict only applies to clothes that *you* purchased. There is a separate set of rules for clothes that are, for all intents and purposes, mementos. Into this subcategory go never-worn gifts from friends, old lovers, and deluded family members.

My mother was a regular supplier to this subcategory because she refused to buy anything that didn't match her personal taste. And since she and I never shared a visual sensibility, she never—even by accident—bought me something I could actually wear. Nevertheless, since it was always clear that she had put time, energy, and thought into the selection of the gift, I felt I couldn't throw it away too quickly.

Brand-new, never-worn items such as these—to which I have some sort of peculiar emotional debt—are subject to their own individual yearly evaluation, based on the degree of discomfort I feel when I imagine them being worn by women in Guatemala, which is where the majority of my clothes wind up, hand-delivered by a woman who used to clean my house. I always get a kick out of picturing a village in Central America full of women dressed in my old Ann Taylor suits with the really big shoulder pads.

After the clothing portion of the purge is accomplished, the really big battles begin. Dealing with the "stuff in my office" is usually like navigating a minefield. Suddenly there are a million different factors to consider. I can't bring myself to throw away anything unusual that I have more than one of, because these could be the early warning signs of a collection. That's why I do not really consider throwing out my two unlikely Pez dispensers or my two three-inch-tall plastic nude women wearing high heels. Certainly not my fast-growing assortment of personalized computer-generated junk mail announcements informing me that I may have won a million dollars. How can I throw away a communication bearing the legend, MERRILL MARKOE! DON'T MAKE US GIVE THE MARKOE MILLION TO SOMEONE ELSE!

Hardest to get rid of are my "reference materials." Sadly for me, I have the broadest possible definition of what a reference material might be. Which is the only explanation I can come up with for saving a story from the April 22, 1980, *National Enquirer* entitled "I Was Nearly Eaten Alive by Thousands of Tiny Sea Lice" and accompanied by a photo of actual sea lice laid side by side near a ruler—proving once and for all that they are in fact as tiny as advertised. To say nothing of the article from a 1982 *Cosmo* entitled "How to Be Delicate," which offers a still-relevant-today list of suggestions, including

"Answer the telephone in a whispery voice" and "Carry a lace-edged hanky (but don't, for heaven's sake, actually *use* it)." And then there's that classic back page from *TV Guide* featuring "John Davidson's Turtle Brownies" ("Now that's incredible!").

This brings me to the several large notebooks labeled MY ACT. They contain the stand-up comedy act I did in the late seventies and early eighties. Stand-up is my one area of nostalgic regret, so at least once a year I take out my act and try it on, much as a better-balanced person might do with an old wedding dress or football uniform. And, as with those things, my act doesn't fit me anymore.

If I were to resume stand-up, I'd have to come up with something a lot more suitable. For instance, my opening line used to go, "I had kind of a sad childhood. I didn't have a date for the senior prom at my high school so my father made my brother take me. But it did turn out okay. My brother and I are getting married. We bought a house in the valley. We're going to settle down and raise mutants." Come to think of it, that used to get a pretty good laugh. Maybe it would be worth trying next time around. Which is what I always say right before I decide to leave the notebooks alone for another year.

And now for the actual cathartic breakthrough of this year's purge. This was the year I threw out my really old love letters. I had three distinct folders from the sixties and seventies that I hadn't looked at in quite some time. I wasn't really sure why I was saving them, except for the vague sense that you don't throw out old love letters. Yet something about them filled me with nonspecific feelings of discomfort. So I sat down and reread them. And being forced to confront the voices of guys from relationships past made me realize what the nonspecific feelings were all about. They were about the real, specific feelings of discomfort that had occasioned the breakups.

Take the letters from a guy I dated sophomore year in college. He was a good-natured blowhard who had a vision of himself as a colorful seafarer. His letters were filled with self-conscious quasi-literary descriptions of his "amazing adventures." That was embarrassing enough, but much worse was reencountering a detail of our relationship that should have remained forgotten. It was that he insisted on calling me Pooh. Nothing I could do or say ever persuaded him to knock it off. Hearing him say it again and again and again in those letters was all I needed to clear a brand-new space in my closet.

Of all the letters I dumped, the funniest were from a guy I spent time with in high school. I had forgotten till the other day that the topic of these letters was a complex analysis of me, intended to convince me to have sex with him. He had me pegged correctly. He knew that his honest, uncomplicated set of reasons had failed him. So his letters were an attempt at psychological analysis the likes of which may not be seen again in our lifetime. Special praise must be given to one poignant paragraph that not only managed to quote each Dylan (both Bob and Thomas) but ended with a unique argument in favor of sex: "It would prepare you," he wrote, "for the riggers [sic] of the life that lies in front of you, both mentally and physically." You have to applaud a guy who comes up with preparation for the "riggers of life" as a way to get a girl into the sack. But not only did I never have sex with him, now I have more room for . . . well . . . for I guess some brand-new reference materials.

HAPPINESS HINT # 25

Come up with an idea
for a new business.

• • •

STUPID OLD
GIRL SCOUTS AGAIN

A couple of weeks ago an article appeared in *The Wall Street Journal* that ripped the lid off something that has been puzzling me for years: the real deal on Girl Scout cookie sales.

But before I elaborate, I would like to share my actual reactions to the Girl Scout experience as recorded in my diary when I was still an active member in the fifth grade.

Thursday Feb. 18
   Today after school went to Girl Scouts. Nothing much happened.

Thursday Feb. 25
   Stupid old Girl Scouts again. We did nothing good as usual.

Friday Feb. 26

Today Mrs. Hoenes called Mrs. Rothhouse and asked why Jill and I didn't seem to be enjoying Girl Scouts. She said we didn't seem to be paying attention during the meetings and that we seemed to be talking to ourselves. Mrs. Rothhouse called Mom and Mom yelled at me and Jill got yelled at too. Mom said we couldn't talk in Girl Scouts anymore. I washed my hair.

Hair washing aside, I was interested to read these diary entries because they provided me with an explanation as to why I couldn't conjure up any specific memories of scouting. This led me to take an informal survey among my now adult female friends to find out what, if anything, *they* remembered about the experience. None of them could remember anything either. In fact, none of us was even sure what was *supposed* to have happened. Something to do with camping, we thought, though we weren't surprised that our moms had all skipped over that part. "We didn't even go outdoors, let alone learn about nature," said my sister-in-law, Anne, who did her tour of duty in St. Louis, Missouri. "In fact, our meetings were held in some kind of underground auditorium." My friend Cynthia, who served in suburban Philadelphia, seems to remember intermittent refreshments. My friend Carol, who did her time in Wisconsin, can only recall that her troop leader had an arm that was easily dislocated and each week the girls in her troop would wait apprehensively to see whether it would be *in* or *out* of its socket. We all kind of liked the idea of the uniforms, for some reason, although some of us worried that they made us look fat. To me, though, Girl Scouts was another boring event that I had to endure, engineered by

well-meaning but dull adults who had no idea how to figure
out anything that might possibly be of interest to bunch of energetic kids after school. Yes, it was all kind of a blank with
one very notable exception.

Friday March 6

Today after school we had our Girl Scout cookie drive.
I had 22 boxes to sell. I had a hard time selling them. Finally, after a long time, Mom took me to the other side of
town where NO Girl Scouts had been yet so I had better
luck there.

Yes, it was the Girl Scout cookie drive.

It was central to being a Girl Scout. Some of us loved the
adult responsibility aspect. My sister-in-law found the experience "terrifying. And the cookies weren't even any good." Not
one of us ever stopped to think where the money we col-
lected was going. Cynthia said she thought she "was helping
to feed starving children." I only knew that *we* didn't get to
keep it. But to me that was just part of being a kid, and I suppose that, on the bright side, we were getting valuable practice at being alienated taxpaying citizens in a country with
an incomprehensible and out-of-control budget. But now I
come to learn that the Girl Scout cookie franchise makes
$400,000,000 a year from what they refer to as "girl-generated
income." "People buy the cookies thinking they are helping
the Girl Scouts, not knowing that the Girl Scouts themselves
only get 40 cents a box" says the article in *The Wall Street
Journal*. And I have to say I find myself unable to figure out
what the troop leader moms even had to show for our forty
cents. Which leads me to believe that it's time for a total re-

vamp of the Girl Scouts in general. How dare they turn well-intentioned, healthy, energetic little girls into terrified pastry salesmen? To say nothing of trapping them in meetings so pointless they must resort to sitting (*without* talking) and waiting for the troop leader to dislocate her shoulder.

Now that we know what kind of money there is to be made in those awful cookies, I suggest we move beyond potentially dangerous door-to-door soliciting into an infomercial featuring testimonials from former Scouts who are now celebs. "I can't really remember what we did at the meetings or anything. And I was always worried that the uniform made me look fat," Cher would say, as they flashed an 800 number to call for cookies, "but now I'm a billionaire, and who is to say that being a Girl Scout played absolutely no part?"

Then I recommend taking this *gigantic* amount of revenue and, by-passing the bogus Girl Scout administrators who apparently get $90,000 a year salaries for doing God only knows what, splitting the profits *evenly* among the *actual troops*. Let the moms use the money to set up programs of real relevance to the lives we now know these little girls will go on to lead. Teach them the stuff they never end up learning anywhere. For instance, how to comprehend the stock market, and the difference between sexual harassment and flirting. Make sure they know what it's *really* like trying to raise a baby all by yourself while working as an office temp. Help them develop a grasp of simple car repairs. Show them a few basic but effective self-defense techniques, including strategies in case you are in an ATM holdup or a carjacking. Explain to them how to understand male doubletalk and how to identify a sociopath before you get involved with him, let alone marry him. Maybe add to that what traits to look for in that more reasonable second husband. Certainly tell them how to start and market their own tastier, more healthful cookie franchise. And how to accessorize a uniform so you don't think you look fat. Then at the end of the year, with the rest of the million or so dollars, take the whole darn bunch to Tahiti for a week. And if they want to talk to their friends during the meetings—I say *let* them.

Take the time to look for
signs of hope.

• • •

It's a
Wonderful Lewis

It was a dark, damp, wintry evening when Lewis wandered
out alone onto the dark, damp, rickety Malibu pier. He had
not announced his departure, just vanished through a hole of
his own construction in the front fence. In the process his collar had come off . . . name tag, rabies tag, everything. He was
untraceable now. Simply gone. History.

He just could no longer think of a valid reason to stay.
Scheduled dining was over for the evening, leaving no hope
for another meal until the next day. Unless Merrill held one of
those spontaneous snack times. Which she frequently did.

He guessed he could have hung around and stared at her
mournfully, allowing long rubbery drools to coagulate in the
corners of his lips. That seemed to encourage her some of the
time. But not all of the time. Maybe that was what finally

drove him to leave. This powerful inconsistent reinforcement was making him insane. He knew he had to get out of there.

Alone, looking down at the waves as they crashed, Lewis was suddenly overcome by the smell of . . . was that food? It beckoned him. "Lewis. Lewis. Come." A wrapper floated by in the murky deep. That was it. He poised himself for a dive.

Just then he became aware of a ghostly presence. Or perhaps it was an angelic one. He had never really absorbed enough television to know the difference. It seemed to have materialized out of a flash of light in the sky. So, unless it was a fly of some kind . . . hmmm, maybe it was a fly. He began to snap at it. But before he could secure it between his teeth, it began to speak.

"Hello, Lewis," the angelic presence said to him. "You're not really thinking about jumping in there, are you?"

"Maybe," said Lewis, ". . . smells like food in there."

"They have a raw sewage problem out here," the angel explained. "That's not really food. Well, it is in a way, but it's too disgusting to talk about. Even to you. Besides, it's *freezing* in there. Not only will you get hepatitis and a host of other dreadful diseases, the tide will pull you out to sea. The undertow will push you down and hold you under."

"Yes," said Lewis, "but it smells like food in there." He poised once again for the jump.

"Wait. Wait. Lewis. Wait. Or maybe I should phrase it this way: *stay*. Before you jump and endanger your life in the name of a poisonous hors d'oeuvre, why not stop and consider what life would be like if you had never been born?"

"Huh? What do you mean?"

"Imagine," said the angel, "a world into which you had

never been born. Let's look in on Merrill. Your mother. Can you see her? Look."

"Yes," said Lewis, suddenly seeing. "There she is. But what's that she's wearing?"

"On her head? Ah, a hat."

"She never wears a hat," said Lewis.

"No," said the angel, "not since you ate them all. But since you were never born, she has a fine assortment of hats. Look. She's taking that one off and putting on another one."

"My God," said Lewis, feeling little globs of drool beginning to form in the corners of his mouth, "and look what she's got on her feet!"

"Yes," said the angel, "those are the suede boots you ate the day she brought you home from the pound. She has several pairs now. In different styles and colors. To match her hats. And the jackets she's not afraid to buy now either."

"The living room looks different," Lewis noticed.

"Yes," said the angel. "More cushions, for one thing. Lots more cushions. The ones you ate, plus a bunch of new ones."

"And what's that in the middle of the room?" Lewis asked.

"That's the antique coffee table she bought with the money she saved on vet bills. Since you were never born, you never got parvo, and she had an extra $1800. And of course, once again, since she didn't have to worry that you would wreck it, she's really enjoying it. Notice how she gazes at it so fondly. And notice all those fragile little crystal items she has displayed on its surface."

"Geez," said Lewis, "and who the hell is *that?*"

"That's her amazingly well behaved new dog, Phil," said the angel. "She got him out of the pound the same day she didn't get you because you had never been born. He's one of those naturally attentive, obedient, smart dogs who doesn't even require a trainer. Look how he sits at her feet and adores her. People are telling her that he could be the next Benji, or Lassie. She's already had offers from movie companies and dog-food manufacturers who are interested in him for commercials."

"I can't take this," said Lewis. "I have to get over there right away. All that extra income will corrupt her. She really *needs* me."

"Go to her, Lewis," said the angel. "Go to her. Return to her life and remind her that materialism is a superficial value. Teach her to cope with loss. Discourage her from being such a damn control freak. Remember, Lewis . . . no dog's life is a failure so long as he still has expensive items to shred."

And so, the angel watched as the big wet dog galumph-galumph-galumphed back to his home.

Increase your knowledge of
something that intrigues you by reading
at least two books on the subject.

• • •

SEX—WHAT, IF ANYTHING, HAVE WE LEARNED?

As someone who lives with the perpetual delusion that there may be important data on even the simplest of everyday topics that only I have neglected to absorb, possibly during those moments in my formal education when I was busy pasting gummed reinforcements over broken holes in my notebook paper instead of paying any sort of real attention, I am the ideal target for every new "how-to" sex, diet, and psychology book to hit the market. Particularly the sex ones. Because of all the areas in which you might like to hear someone's advice, sex provides the most perfect mirror for your insecurities. Hardly anyone discusses it that openly. Someone, anyone, might know some secrets you don't. That's what I always figure.

Toward that end, I've purchased an assortment of sex

books at various points in my life. In the seventies it was *The Joy of Sex,* the book that tried to tame and package for public consumption such then-fringe erotica as provocative lingerie and light bondage. It was most memorable for its excruciatingly detailed line drawings of a moderately attractive heterosexual couple doing every conceivable thing to each other. The male half looked kind of like the aging Eric Clapton, while the bubble hairstyle and blue eyeshadow on the female gave her a faint resemblance to a young Elizabeth Taylor. At least, right up until that moment when your eye traveled downward to discover her vast quantity of proudly displayed sixties counterculture-style armpit hair.

When I first got the book, I remember contemplating the woman's defiantly unvain boxy shape as she cavorted around in a push-up bra and garter belt and thinking to myself "Wow—if someone is willing to find *her* sexy, looking like *that,* I guess I have nothing to worry about." And then, of course, I started to worry seconds later, "My God. What if I bought an outfit like that and *I* looked that bad?" That was the end of my thoughts about purchasing any push-up bras or garter belts for at least a decade.

My search for helpful hints continued into the eighties when I bought a book with a bright gold cover called *Great Sex* by Alexandra Penney. The problem with this one came in the author's interspersed fantasy scenarios. For example, this typical excerpt: " 'Look how wonderful your apartment is,' he exclaimed, still clasping her tightly to him while his keen eyes measured the room. 'You didn't tell me you were such a good cook.' and . . . suddenly he was there, his two hands holding her face up to be kissed." I kind of gave up hope for any good advice from this book right then and there. This was not about *my* life. Not only have I never, at any point, been the recipient of a "two-handed face-holding kiss," but a fantasy night of sex and romance hinging on a guy being bowled over by my wonderful apartment and my incredible cooking is harder for me to imagine than my own willingness to risk looking dorky in lingerie and a push-up bra. That's the problem with sex books: Since they're always written by people, you have to find one by someone who's a lot like you.

So far in the nineties there have been two well-publicized entries in the "is anyone ever going to give some *real* advice" sex book sweepstakes.

First there was the irresistibly titled "How to Satisfy a Woman EVERY Time . . . and Have Her Beg for More," which interested me immediately because I am a woman who has not necessarily been satisfied EVERY time. (I'm not pointing any fingers.) Sadly, the "how-to" advice in the title turns out to be about "teasing" a woman by entering her only a little bit at a time. ("Don't ever go in all the way until she starts having an orgasm. As much as you are teasing her you are teasing yourself too.") Not much of a revelation. But the author's *real* secret seems to be how to turn a sensationalist title and the aforementioned tiny bit of questionable data into a 123-page book by piecing together 113 other pages from bits of *The Hite Report* and *Penthouse* "Forum." To say nothing of her impressive ability to expound endlessly on such breakthrough notions as "a healthy body is a loving body," which then leads into an entire chapter on vitamins and culminates in an 800 number that allows interested readers to purchase the author's special "energy shake." Not much insight about sex, but a good lesson in merchandising.

Which brings us to the much hyped *Sex* by Madonna. And

it's not as if I think I have nothing to learn from Madonna. She is not only more successful than I am in every measurable way, but all two hundred of her newly minted "looks" seem to work better for her than my one enduring look has ever worked for me.

"These are fantasies I have dreamed up," she tells us as the book begins. An interesting idea: the world's first self-employed centerfold. A woman who is not just the object of the fantasy but also the architect. "I'll teach you how to fuck," it says in big letters on the next page. Okay. I'll take some pointers. But what appears on the opposite page—a full-page photo of Madonna in a nippleless studded leather bikini (very much like the one I wear to swim laps) and a black mask, sucking on her own finger—is a perfect indication of the kind of thing Madonna has to teach. You don't have to venture too much further into the contents to have it occur to you that nothing turns Madonna on like the chance to be alone with Madonna.

Complete and total narcissism is the only message of *Sex*. For Madonna, not only do sexual feelings involve other people watching her be preoccupied with herself, but she almost always makes sure that she is the only person of identifiable sexuality in any of her pictorials. All the people in her world are geeks. Well, this is true for me too, but *her* geeks are men who look like women, women who look like carnival workers, and zombies, and Vanilla Ice, who is kind of a combination of all of the above.

One of the book's big centerpieces is a three-way encounter featuring model Naomi Campbell and rapper Big Daddy Kane. In it, Madonna, dressed only in a pair of polka-dotted bikini bottoms, sits with her legs apart and her head thrust back dramatically. Her eyes are closed, her makeup is perfect, her Ursula Andress "fall" cascading down her back. She is touching no one. No one touches her. Shhh. If we listen very carefully we can hear the steamy conversation they were having just before the picture was taken. Shhhhhh.

BIG DADDY KANE: What do I do? Just stand right here like this? And do nothing?

MADONNA: Everyone! Attention! Is the hairpiece okay? Will someone please check the hairpiece and see if it's okay?

HAIR PERSON: Yes. Incredible! It's absolutely incredible. We are ready to go. Wait! Freeze one more second? Someone! She needs lips.

MAKEUP PERSON: I'm right here. Lips, and cheeks, and . . . perfect.

MADONNA: How about lashes?

MAKEUP: Lashes are fabulous. Fabulous.

BIG DADDY KANE: And I still just stand here like this? And do nothing? You sure? You just want me to stand right here and do *nothing?*

NAOMI CAMPBELL: Shhh. What are you griping about? Your paycheck is gonna clear. Be quiet.

After reading this book, I come away with two important thoughts.

1. The book Madonna is really meant to write is called *Money*. That will be the one with the sexy, exciting photos.

2. I hope someone told her that "if honey pours from [her] gash" again, she should run, not walk, to a urologist for some amoxycillin. Sounds to me like she has a urinary tract infection.

Afterword

Three decades of perusing how-to sex books have convinced me that I am finally in possession of all the REALLY VALUABLE KEYS TO ACHIEVING ECSTASY. And if you write to me in care of this publisher and enclose $19.95 (plus postage and handling) I will be happy to send you my own special 123-page book that explains in vivid detail not only how what *I* have learned can change *your* life, but also includes a delightful recipe for my trademark Holiday Cheese Puffs at no extra cost to you.

HAPPINESS HINT # 28

Risk meeting people in
brand-new ways.

• • •

THE SOULMATE DIARIES

There is a specific point at which you shift from being recently single to really single. It comes when you have heard this piece of advice more than twice: "Well, you have to get OUT THERE." At first it sort of means something to you. "Yes," you think, "that's right. That's my problem. I have to get out there." This occurs immediately before you find yourself unable to answer the question: "Out *where?*" And of course the people who gave you this advice cannot tell you where OUT THERE is. They have no idea. They are the same people who probably also said to you, "One door closes. Another door opens." "*What* door?" you probably wondered. The door that goes OUT THERE.

When you're in your early twenties, everywhere you happen to be *is* out there. By the time you hit your middle thirties, the location of out there is getting kind of vague, and by your late thirties and early forties you're mainly worried that it's going to be a long drive. I read in a book that the female eel travels 1500 miles on land and sea to mate. I myself currently get depressed when I realize I have to go all the way to Santa Monica.

And even after you have made some decision about where "out there" is, you may still find yourself puzzled by what it is you're supposed to do when you arrive out there. Do you just show up looking fetching, batting your eyes at everyone? And how long do you have to keep this up before you get to go back inside?

These were not actually the questions on my mind the day I stumbled (or perhaps was guided) to the self-help section of my local video rental establishment. On that day I was filled with the kind of self-loathing that comes from having actually contemplated renting a Steven Seagal movie. So disgusted was I with myself that I felt I should at least *look* at the educational shelf of the store. Not that I found anything educational per se. I decided to try two tapes. The first one was called *Attracting Prosperity*. In it Louise L. Hay, a bleached-blond woman in her fifties, was addressing a moderate-sized audience of her followers. She began by assuming the Christ-on-the-Cross position as she led the group in this affirmation: "I am open and receptive to all good." Then she told us to take out "our precious little mirrors that are so wonderful" for some "mirror work." As we gazed adoringly at our own reflections, we were asked to complete the following sentence: "My biggest fear about money is . . ." While I was still deciding on my answer, someone with a microphone went out into the audience to gather a sampling of opinions.

The camera closed in on a bearded guy in a sweater who was having trouble "attracting a new house." I recognized him. It was Larry. The man who fixes my sprinklers! That was it for me. I wasn't ready to spend the evening confronting Larry's house-hunting problems.

So I started tape number two. *Attracting Love Through Self-Hypnosis*.

"Find the ways to reach the soulmate of your dreams," it said on the box. "Dick Sutphen [a man who has never even *seen* my sprinklers as far as I know] offers two methods of subliminal programming."

What follows are the diaries that recorded my attempts to follow his advice.

Dear Diary:

This is an extremely powerful tape. At least that's what the voice on the tape tells me right from the very beginning as I watch computer-generated blips on black go whizzing by me like a very inexpensively made version of *Star Wars*. The disembodied voice of Dick Sutphen pretty much guarantees me that I am going to enter a hypnotic state that will allow me to break down the barriers to my subconscious and superconscious. This will allow him to reprogram me so that I "draw my soulmate."

If I do this properly I think at last I will have a workable solution to what I am supposed to do when I am OUT THERE. The answer will be: NOTHING! I can just relax, have a beer, take a nap . . . because now my newly programmed unconscious will be doing it FOR ME!!! This is exactly the kind of breakthrough I was hoping for.

Attracting Love

DAY ONE: Getting "OUT THERE" with my friend Carol.

My friend Carol and I eat dinner out together quite a bit. But this time, before we leave, I force her to undergo soulmate attraction self-hypnosis with me. I am anxious to see what kind of effect the simultaneous powers of our unconscious minds *both* drawing soulmates will have on our combined dining experience.

We watch the tape in her living room. It is a tribute to the comfort level of our friendship that we are both able to play along with the "repeat technique" section which is "designed to communicate to every level of the body and mind" without laughing derisively. We have seen each other through stupider things than this. Well, not *much* stupider. Actually, this may be the stupidest thing. But nevertheless we both begin to chant along in earnest, "I am ready for a loving relationship and I use the unlimited powers of my mind to draw my soulmate to me." (And then, a little later in the tape, "I now manifest a warm fulfilling soulmate relationship in my life and so it is.")

When we finish, Carol confesses she was having trouble concentrating, although she thought the melding blobs section of the video was kind of sexy. I, on the other hand, felt I had done quite a good job of communicating with the deepest fibers of my being. And as we head out for a restaurant we both like in the Malibu area I actually do feel relaxed and glad to be alive, like Dick Sutphen promised. I am optimistic. Recently Carol and I have had a number of dining mishaps, due to the fact that everywhere we eat we are being seated directly next to one or another of her old boyfriends. It proves disruptive and we have to leave, but now that we are able to communicate through "the powers of unconditional love" I feel this will no longer be a problem.

Almost the minute we are seated a handsome, well-dressed guy comes over to say hello to her. He is age appropriate. He looks successful and intriguing. I am very impressed. Carol greets him and follows him over to his table where I cannot hear the conversation, but I can see that he is introducing her to the people he is with. They chat for a while longer. Wow. This soulmate stuff is really something. "Who was that?" I ask enviously when she finally returns. "My ex-husband," she whispers through gritted teeth. "I think I may kill him. Do you mind if we change restaurants?"

Well, an ex-husband. That's closer to a soulmate than a simple ex-boyfriend. I decide to think this is a good sign.

We head across the street to an Italian place. As we walk in the door, Pierce Brosnan is beating a hasty retreat, apparently too chicken to risk even being within striking distance of the unlimited powers of my mind. Okay, fine with me. I never thought he was my soulmate anyway.

We sit down at a table and within seconds of our arrival the front door of the restaurant opens and in walk two people who I know do not like me. They immediately spot me and feel obligated to come over and greet me. They are pretending that nothing is wrong, speaking in high-pitched tones of voice that tell me they are uncomfortable and wish this had never happened.

Suddenly it occurs to me that not only are Carol and I not drawing any soulmates, we are drawing a lot of people with whom we have bad karma. We decide we had better put the unlimited powers of our minds on ice for a while or at this rate we might never get anything to eat.

DAY TWO: Getting "OUT THERE" with my friend Robin.
"I feel like a complete goofball," Robin says to me as she tries to be a good sport about the chanting. But I can tell she isn't fully buying into the unlimited powers of her mind like I am. This time *I* am going whole hog.

Afterward we go to a big, noisy, popular seafood restaurant across the highway from the ocean. About a half hour into our fish tacos, a nice-looking guy comes up to me. "Are you Merrill?" he asks. He doesn't look familiar. But he *is* kind of attractive. He turns out to be a guy that a mutual friend once tried to fix me up with. He actually phoned my house a few times. I didn't return his calls. In fact, I am haunted by the vague sense that I wasn't particularly nice to him. "Good to see you again," I say, growing increasingly ill at ease. "What had I said to that guy?" I keep asking myself as I wolf down my dinner. I'm glad I can't remember. Time for another premature departure. These unlimited powers of my mind are getting very annoying. Though, on the bright side, they are turning out to be a pretty good weight loss program.

DAY THREE: Getting "OUT THERE" with my friend Cynthia.
One more chance. That's all I'm giving the damn unlimited powers. After that they can just talk to my lawyer. So next I force Cynthia to submit to soulmate hypnosis. We

are seated in her bedroom and all five of her dogs are staring at us. She clearly feels like a goose. *I* am convinced that the third time's a charm. By the time we get to the part where we are counting backwards and "going deeper, deeper, deeper, down down down" I am positive I'm going to make these powers work for me or someone is going to get hurt. And sure enough—we are barely finished with the giving and receiving unconditional love section when all five of her dogs run to the front door and start to bark. There were probably soulmates on the porch. One of us really should have at least gotten up to go check.

Afterward we head out to a restaurant on Ventura Boulevard in Studio City. It is a crowded, lively place where the tables are so close to each other that if we draw any soulmates we will have to be very careful that they don't spill anything on us.

The tape does seem to have had an effect on Cynthia. She immediately develops unconditional love for a man at the next table. Unfortunately he is wearing a wedding ring. But she doesn't let that dampen her spirits. Seconds later she is intrigued by our middle-aged busboy. Her inexplicable attraction to him causes him to stare at us in a way that begins to make me queasy. It occurs to me that it's a good thing the tape didn't tell her that she was a sea bass or she might be flopping around on the floor right now, gasping for air.

Meanwhile I notice that only one table away a pudding-faced Rick Dees, seated with his wife and son, is glumly finishing up his meal. I thank God that he has his family with him, helping to distract him from my amazing powers. Because I have never been a fan of his and, so help me, if he had come over to our table, I would have had to turn the dump over.

Just before we leave, as I wait at the bar while Cynthia goes to the ladies' room, the bartender begins to confess to me the hatred he has for his job. The pay is bad. The hours are endless. He has really beautiful blue eyes. Whiny, angry, and cute: looks like a soulmate to me. At least he wasn't anyone I already knew and hated. I decided to call that progress. And the end to the soulmate experiment. Time to see if there's something better to do with the unlimited powers of my mind. Maybe see if they can attract a cure for cancer or AIDS. Guess I'll head back to the video rental place and see if there's a tape for that.

And if there's not, maybe this time I'll have the courage to tune back in and see how Larry the sprinkler guy did attracting a house.

Read a section of a newspaper or
magazine that you ordinarily skip.

• • •

NEW THINGS
TO WORRY ABOUT

A few weeks ago I was taking a shower when I heard myself
begin a new line of worrying. This is not out of character for
me. (And, by the way, neither is showering. I have excellent
hygiene. Ask anyone.) But the inspiration for this brand-new
avenue of self-torture was the recent spate of reports regard-
ing breast implant tragedies and mishaps. As I was soaping up
(and, for you trivia buffs, this is officially the only moment of
full frontal nudity you'll find in my books), I heard myself fret-
ting as follows: "Oh, brother. Next thing I know I'll wake up
in the morning and my breasts will be all sore and infected
and then they'll begin to harden and my nipples will hurt and
I'll have to go in to have surgery to try and scrape out the leak-
ing silicone." And only *after* I had worked myself up into

quite a state did I remember, "Oh, that's right. I never *had*
breast implants."

I believe it was Franklin Roosevelt who spoke the immortal
words, "The only thing we have to fear is fear itself." Boy, oh
boy, what an understatement. Fear itself is *plenty*. Particularly
in the special wee hours of the morning when every little
problem comes to visit in a form that seems hideously unsolvable. This is the time of night when you get the karmic pay-
back for having consumed too many tabloid-style talk and
news shows. For example, the other night it began to occur to
me that I seem to be the only semineurotic woman in America
who was *never* an incest victim—or that maybe I really *am*
one and the horrifying flashbacks just haven't come to me yet.
After all, that's what the 250,000 different incest victims that
I've seen interviewed on Oprah, Phil, Geraldo, Sally Jessy,
"Hard Copy," "Inside Edition," "A Current Affair," "60 Minutes," "20/20," and "MTV's House of Style" all said. And if it
does turn out that I am the only remaining person in America
who never had sex with her father, what does that say about
me? What am I, chopped liver? So unappealing that even my
own father rejected me, now leaving me clueless as to how to
find the appropriate sociological cliché that can get me into a
category on "The Montel Williams Show"? (Hey! Maybe that *is*
a category!)

This is when it occurred to me that modern life has provided us with whole new areas for worry—obsessional topics
never even dreamed possible by our turn-of-the-century fore-
bears. They had to make do with basic, primitive fears such as
drought, famine, flood, plague, avalanche, ambush by really
irate Native Americans, untimely death due to much shorter

life span. . . . Come to think of it, there has *always* been a wonderful variety of reasons for terror and anxiety.

A FEW BRAND-NEW THINGS I HAVE FOUND TO WORRY ABOUT

1. That I will wake up one morning to find that I am half of one of those couples I keep seeing in commercials who have heartfelt, earnest talks about breakfast cereal, and who actually share special moments discussing raisins.

2. That everything we currently think of as love is not so much a transcendent, binding emotion as it is a kind of chemical imbalance. Certain studies indicate that the principal force of attraction between a romantically inclined male and a romantically inclined female is, simply, scent. This can be such a powerful force that it is actually used as a form of birth control in cockroaches. Dousing the male cockroach with the scent of the female gets him so excited he begins to run in circles and is unable to have sex. As any single woman will tell you, bringing about this type of behavior in human males sometimes takes months of tedious social activities and relationship discussions. So I guess we can all look for the day when men will be able to go through all the motions of dating just by dousing themselves with some kind of extract, eventually never having to bother springing for dinner and a movie.

And, as a corollary, I am also beginning to worry that before the year is out, I will have read so many pop-psychology books about the personality dysfunctions of the human male that I will be able to identify my dates by title, chapter heading, and page number before the appetizers have been cleared away.

3. That I will never again understand enough about the constantly re-forming boundaries of Eastern European countries to appear even superficially informed—a mode that, quite frankly, has served me well for at least two decades. That forevermore I will be at gatherings of smart people whose approval I seek, and just as I have proudly figured out a way not only to pronounce Azerbaijan but to use it in a sentence, they will also look at me with barely concealed disdain and say, "No, no, dear. You must be thinking of Tajikistan." So I will go home and figure out what it is I am supposed to appear to know about Tajikistan, only to learn moments later that it has decided to merge with Nagorno-Karabakh.

4. The idea of death, in its many and varied forms, has long been the staple of the worrier—always there for us when things seem to be going well in other areas. But now comes this new wrinkle on the landscape: *the threat of eternal life.* Scientists have predicted that in the not-too-distant future an average human life will span about 300 years. If society adjusts its current priorities proportionately, this means we may all be forced to attend high school until we are in our seventies! Not only will it end up being illegal to purchase liquor until we are in our eighties, but there's reason to believe that adolescent identity crisis as well as its accompanying angst-ridden behaviors will continue until then as well. If that isn't daunting enough, imagine trying to keep the sex in a marriage fresh for *a century.* To say nothing of trying to decide how many pairs of each new style of clothing we ought to buy, knowing that the style will be back dozens and dozens of more times, always at higher prices. And then there's the number of remakes of *It's a Wonderful Life* for which we would have to pretend enthusiasm, to say nothing of the sheer quantity of "Cheers" reruns to which an individual would be subjected—it all adds up to a very good reason to not bother to look both ways before crossing the street.

5. That by the millennium the Christmas season will be officially ten months long. I already have begun to worry about its onset on the Fourth of July—a date that always means that before you know it summer will have fluttered by like a crumpled tissue in a stiff breeze, and the big fat guys will start putting up the fencing around their pumpkin/Christmas tree lots. Year after year my campaigns for an alternate-year Christmas gift-giving plan go unheeded. All I ask is that in "even" years we obey the edicts we hear constantly about "honoring the true spirit of Christmas in our hearts." Only. Period. Then in the *odd*-numbered years, when gift-giving is back as a tradition, we'll all be glad to see it again. Maybe.

6. That something spectacularly good or uniquely horrible will happen and—blammo!—I'm the topic of a TV movie. Because no matter who you are, no matter what your story, of one thing you can be certain: the networks will figure out a way to make sure you're played by Barbara Eden.

Brainstorm with a friend about
alternative careers.

• • •

SECRETS OF THE
LOVE TRADE

Perhaps the goofiest job I ever had was demonstrating vibrators at Sears one Christmas. I was supposed to get the attention of holiday shoppers by touching them lightly on the arm or shoulder with my humming hand-held vibration device. Then I was supposed to interest them in a discussion, or possible purchase, of same in the demonstration area that was conveniently located nearby. After only a couple of dead-eye stares from harried and unamused Sears patrons who did not wish to have their progress impeded by a girl with a buzzing hand, I became too skittish to continue.

Tying for the second goofiest job is almost all the work I have ever done in television. Without a doubt Los Angeles is the goofy-job capital of the country. There are people who make movable, radio-controlled dead-body facsimiles for a living. There are people who add prerecorded laughter to performances that could never have inspired an actual audience to actual laughter. There's the job that made Vanna White a beloved international star. And there's the job my friend Mimi Pizzi had for four months when she was a writer of the dates on "The Love Connection."

For readers too snotty or effete to watch prime-time trash TV, "The Love Connection" is a long-running hit game show whose premise picks up where "The Dating Game," another long-time favorite, left off. On the show, volunteers select a partner from videos of dating candidates, and the show sends the two of them out on a date, all expenses paid, on the understanding that afterward both halves of the couple will come back on the show and fill everyone in on all the gory details.

I found myself growing sort of semi-fascinated by the show last winter when my own love life had become turbulent and horrifying. I was intrigued and even faintly comforted by the fact that I could turn on the television and witness total strangers who apparently had been out on dates and lived to tell about it. It was also heartening that they seemed to feel there were rules to be obeyed, expectations to be met or not met. As a person whose social life was in chaos, I felt that this gave the semblance of order to the universe. That anyone might work as a "writer" on the show never occurred to me until I met Mimi. Since she was planning a job change, she agreed to let me come and witness her labors at "The Love Connection" before she left it in the proverbial dust.

Here's how it all happens. Before the people who go out on the dates get to the show itself they are interviewed, videotaped and matched up with potential choices by various staff members. And then, before the actual date, they receive a letter telling them what's required. "Remember that the concept of our show is to simply ascertain the events and honest opinions of a couple who have been matched by videotape," it explains. "What you do on the date is up to you or the person who selected you. But events that allow you and your date to get to know each other result in much more interesting segments on the show." Toward this end, the letter goes on to say, "Please do *not* go to any of the following: Sea World, Catalina Island, theater or movies, comedy clubs, dinner mystery shows or amusement parks." I, for one, wish someone would distribute a letter like this to those of us in real life who must date. "Just before your taping," the letter goes on, "you will be reminded of the details of your date." This is where Mimi comes in.

Her week starts out with a series of phone calls. "Typically on any Monday I'll get six new couples," Mimi tells me. "The priority is to talk to as many of them as you can and get each person's opinion of the date. Then you rate the date as a G (good) or an NG (no good)."

Mimi says she calls "the select*or*" first. Backstage at "The Love Connection," they refer to the two people on the date as the *"or"* and the *"ee."* "I feel so voyeuristic," Mimi confesses, "when I'm listening to these people and I have to ask them questions I don't really want the answers to.

"One of the very first dates I had was this older couple. He was, like, sixty. She was fifty-five. And he was saying what a great kisser he was. Women would tell him, 'Tom, your kisses are just magic.' So my producer wanted me to ask him what about his kissing was so magical. So I say, 'What about your technique is it?' and he says, 'Well, I just give 'em a little pressure with my tongue, just a little resistance,' and I'm sitting there thinking, *I don't want to know this.*"

After interrogating both participants, Mimi organizes their thoughts for them on paper. And right before the taping, she takes the *"or"* into a briefing room and, in her words, "I'll be holding this thing, and I'll say, 'This is not a script.' It is a script, though. So I'll go through it with them and then I'll say, 'Okay, spit it back to me,' and depending on how good their memories are, how good their delivery is, they may go over it once, twice, or three times." This is the life of a writer on "The Love Connection."

As with all people who hold eccentric jobs, Mimi just kind of fell into this date-writing business. It was never a long- or a short-term goal for her. After a childhood spent in Minnesota watching a lot of TV, Mimi majored in speech and communications in college and then started on a series of goofy media jobs. Before "The Love Connection" she had been producing segments for the "Home" show. "Every day there were a couple of celebrities who had to *do* something," she says. "So basically I would make up tips for people who didn't have any. Like Alley Mills, who cohosted the show for a week. Alley doesn't cook. But they wanted her to cook, and it was Cinco de Mayo, so, by God, she was going to make something Mexican. I found a salsa recipe for Alley, and I had to teach her how to make it. I said to her, 'Make it sound like you've been doing this salsa recipe for years.' So she did. And a mariachi band came out and played at the end, and nobody gave a shit."

Eventually Mimi became fed up with segments in which "someone came out and told you how to build a log cabin out of bread sticks and Cheez Whiz," and then an old friend offered her the "Love Connection" job. "I had heard thousands of horror stories," she says. "Everyone I ever met said don't go. But you go anyway." (People who work in television aren't put off by dire warning because they know it's *all* pretty weird.) "I showed up at their studio and watched someone do a briefing, and I laughed and thought, *This is fun. It's better than asking Linda Kelsey to show us how to wash sweaters.*"

And so it came to pass that Mimi became a writer of dates and a bearer of specific knowledge about the working of same. "Men more than women will put a good face on the date," for example. Mimi noticed that the men would often just skate through their description of the date. But a woman would say, "He was cheap! He ignored me! He used me as a showpiece!"

Mimi finds this the weirdest aspect of her date-writing job. "I'll talk to two people, and one of them thinks they had a nice time while the other thinks it sucked. And nine times out of ten it's the man who didn't measure up and had no clue," she notes. "So you call the guy back and say, 'Mary doesn't want to go out with you again. And these are some of the things she's gonna say.' And you sort of hope that he gets incensed and starts spitting stuff back at you because you don't want one person to just roll over the other."

When I went backstage to watch her in action, I saw how right she was. There was this guy in his thirties who "thought things went okay" when he took his date to the state fair. "I just kind of figured maybe she was having an off day," he said stoically. "I'd take her out again." But then, when he and the woman in question hit the air, the woman was rolling her eyes a lot and consumed by displeasure. "Women are less afraid to tell the truth," Mimi said. "Men don't want to look bad on television."

I should say here that Mimi is a compassionate writer. "I try to pump these guys up about bad dates," she explained to me. "I'm kind of ashamed to say this, but I told one guy that if he acted like a wimp on television he would never date again. And he was in a room full of guys who had had bad dates. So it was kind of like the huddle at a football game, with the guys all slapping him on the ass before he went out to do his spot. It really got him going."

Mimi said she thought that black women were the most entertaining on the show because they were so refreshingly direct with their disappointments. "Black women who have had a bad date will *kill* the guy. They don't give a damn," she said admiringly. I myself witnessed an instance of this when I met an irate black woman who was just chock-full of exasperating details of all the things she had suffered in the name of social life. The guy she'd gone out with was affable but basically under the impression that things hadn't gone too badly. Then Mimi carefully explained that the woman was planning to take him apart limb from limb. "So that's how it is," he said, comprehending for the first time what would happen when the camera began taping, "She wants a bloodbath." By the time he was ready to go on, Mimi had helped him prepare a story that would stand up to his date's.

After the taping was over, she turned to me and said, "Working on this kind of show means you never want to have a first date again." Of course that's the deal with a good dumb job—it leaves you with a permanent scar. My waitressing job has made me forever edgy in coffee shops. My sitcom-writing job made me stop watching most prime-time TV. And this is probably why I will never take a job as a restaurant critic, a wine taster, or a high-priced call girl. Well, a restaurant critic anyway.

Go out and attend a
state fair or a circus.

• • •

WHAT I DID ON
MY SUMMER VACATION

Perusing the things-to-do section of the newspaper, I was
taken by a little drawing of happy cows riding on a roller
coaster. "Don't miss *your* San Fernando Fair," it said. "We're
on the Mooove." If *cows* could enjoy the damn thing, I rea-
soned, so could I.

And so it came to pass that I left my even-temperatured
home near the beach to venture into the scorching heat of the
San Fernando Valley in search of the "Livestock, Home Arts
Exhibits, Gardening, Arts and Crafts and Continuous Entertainment" that I was assured of finding at *my* Fair.

Now, the San Fernando Valley is a vast, unbroken stretch of
affluent suburbs, often enshrouded in smog. It's bordered on
one edge by Ventura Boulevard, an industrial strip, stretching
as far as the eye can see, with single-story businesses on both

sides of the road: car dealerships; lighting-fixture emporiums; frozen yogurt and chocolate chip cookie franchises; mini-malls, each with a Radio Shack and a 7-Eleven; more car dealerships; more lighting-fixture emporiums; on and on ad infinitum.

While there are many associations to be made with the San Fernando Valley, quilting bees and 4-H exhibits are pretty far down on the list. Which of course is why I wanted to check the thing out—a decision that I couldn't help but question when I stepped out of my car into what must have been 350° heat.

Ah, the fair! What a cavalcade of sensory stimuli! Everywhere, sweating red-faced men in baseball caps and T-shirts that don't fully cover their bellies are forcing fun on small children whose love they are trying to buy because they only get to see them on alternate weekends since the divorce. And the smells! DOG COOKED ON A STICK! is the first big sign I see on a refreshment booth—an interesting lesson in how critical the word *hot* can be to the appetite. Inside, teenage girls whose faces redefine forever the phrase *the depths of human boredom* stare glassy-eyed at a giant pan of wienies baking under a light bulb.

With no sign of quaint agrarian activities anywhere, I head into the midway, where I ponder the question, Can an unaccompanied female (even a professionally peculiar one like me) maintain any vestigial sense of dignity or cool when riding around strapped into a tiny car? I learn that the answer is no after boarding the Haunted House and seeing the look two teenagers on a date give me after they are forced to sit down right in front of me. It's the face I used to make when I was forced to attend social activities with my parents.

But wait! Beyond the Avon booth, in back of NATURE'S ODOR GUARD—THE SOLUTION TO ODOR POLLUTION, there's the building that holds the *fair* part of the fair. And sure enough, inside there *is* a quilt! Not only that, a tabletop full of Saran-Wrapped pound cakes and brownies, some of which have apparently won prizes! Elsewhere there is even a display of what look to be fairly standard issue vegetables (the category of which I imagine to be Best Shopping by a Housewife in a National Grocery Chain).

Okay, so maybe *my* San Fernando Valley Fair *does* come up short in the canning and pie-baking departments. But if you went to the fair in Nebraska, could you enter the John Casablancas Be-a-Model Makeover Contest or have a "free spinal screening" by a chiropractor? And so in summing up the experience I would like to quote from the indigenous poetry of the fair, as seen in a sign at one of the rides I was too embarrassed to go on by myself. YOU HAVE TO BE AS TALL AS THIS FENCE/TO SLIDE ALONE, it said—and I don't think Bob Dylan could have explained it any better.

FREE SCREEN TEST

That's what the ad in the giveaway newspaper said. ACT IN MOTION PICTURES, TV. BEGINNERS WANTED—WE TRAIN. Why not, for God's sake? This is L.A.!

So I find myself walking into a storefront. Just across from a mortuary, on a Hollywood street. Inside, the receptionist, a fiftyish woman with dark, pinned-up hair, motions for me to sit on a couch flanked by two plastic palm trees. The room is heavily decorated with paintings of Elvis and a few 8-by-10 glossies of women in swimwear and high heels shaking hands with men, none of whom I can identify. The receptionist is talking to a big, good-looking guy in his thirties about how she used to dance professionally with Mario Lanza when a young black woman with dreadlocks is ushered out of an inner office and I am instructed to go in.

Inside, a stocky white-haired man is seated at a desk. "My, what a pretty girl you are," he says to me. "Do you think you could handle leading parts in pictures?" Immediately I am impressed by his good taste and judgment. "We're a studio," he tells me. "We just make one picture after another. We've been here since 1938. I'm eighty-one years old. I've been directing and producing since I was seventeen. You could do commercials." Then he tells me, "You're a young stewardess type. Would you like to earn $1,000 to $1,200 a week?" "Well, okay," I say, adjusting immediately to my new role as media whore.

"It's a government school," he tells me. "The whole course is $600, but the government pays the whole thing. It's called grants." "I don't get it," I tell him. "Doing a commercial is paid for by a government grant?" I ask about the screen test. "That's just for beginners," he says. "Why don't I have you try out for speaking parts? I can see you're ready to work. I want you to read this skit with that young man out there." Then he hands me a three-page scene from something called *Saturday's Children*, written for two characters named Bobby and Rims. "What can you tell me about the character I'm playing?" I ask. "Her name is Bobby. She's a woman," he says as he shows me into a dilapidated back room full of motel-art-type paintings. The big, good-looking guy is already back there. "You two read this together. Then I'll be back to take a look at you," he tells us.

So we begin to rehearse the scene, which sounds as if it was written in the thirties because of its oddly dated turns of phrase, such as, "Oh, Rims, dear, don't you get tired of poor me? Ever?" My scene partner, although clearly all-American, reads English as though it is his second language. Even after six rehearsals, our scene still falls short—not what you might call entertainment. Suddenly the receptionist bursts in. "It's eventually all going back to radio," she tells us firmly. "It *has* to. In TV everyone has to be so glamorous, but in radio you can show up with your hair in curlers. Although I wouldn't advise it because sometimes there *is* a small audience."

Now she hands us another scene to read. It's called *Wilderness Wife*. "In the wilderness of northern Ontario stands a little log cabin," my partner, who is now the narrator, reads in a voice that sounds like he's coming out of a heavy anesthesia. "And inside, Myra Webster is making some meat pies. Way off in the distance a man plobs his way toward the cabin."

"Plows," the receptionist corrects him. "I made a mistake when I typed this."

"When he reaches her side, he drops a bundle of beaver pelts, puts his arm around her and kisses her," the narrator continues, and begins to move toward me. "You don't have to touch," the receptionist interjects. "*Real* actors can get their point across without ever touching anyone." Before we can get our point across she suggests that we accompany her backstage. "I'd like to show you a few things," she says, as I think I hear the theme from "The Twilight Zone." "Usually I work for Rockwell on the B-1 bomber," the big guy enthuses as we return to a stage area that is decorated with a green Naugahyde couch and two little paintings of pixies. "Now I want each of you to get up onstage and say why you want to be an actor," she says. Lucky for me the big guy gets right up.

"The reason I want to be an actor is that it seems like an interesting field," he says. "Okay, now do a little scene," the receptionist tells him. "Act something out." The big guy pauses, turns his profile to us, and addresses two imaginary people. "I think you've both had enough to drink," he says, "and now I'm going to have to ask you to leave." Turning back to us, he explains, "I used to be a bouncer." "Very good!" says the receptionist, spearheading the applause. It's been two hours and I still have no idea where this is leading, so I mention that I have another appointment. "Well, please talk to the director on your way out," the receptionist instructs me, turning all her attention to the big guy.

The "director" is sitting alone in his office, hidden behind piles of paper on his desk. "I didn't realize you were such a dynamic actress," he says to me. "You could sell anything. Phone sales. You ever do that?" "No," I say, frankly crushed that I have been demoted from leading lady to telephone salesperson in no time at all. "Well, I'm going to get you some work," he promises me. "You'd be perfect for a show like 'L.A. Law.' And I think I have a picture for you." "What kind of picture?" I asked him. "Super 8," he says. "Can you be reached evenings after seven?" I tell him I can. "I was also interested in that big boy out there," he says to me. "How's he doing?" "Well," I say, "he's fine. Except he doesn't have any idea of how to read lines." " 'L.A. Law,' " the guy says to me. "I'm gonna get him on 'L.A. Law.' " And I never heard from any of them again.

Order a gift for yourself
from a catalog.

• • •

THE WEEK OF NOT JUST FEELING GREAT BUT *BEING* GREAT

Like most red-blooded American citizens, I get a lot of catalogs in the mail. I usually don't scrutinize them too carefully
unless I have a writing deadline, in which case I suddenly feel
compelled to read the description of every colorful gift de-
canter and pair of pressed wool slacks. In fact, it was on one
such perusal of the J. Crew catalog that I made the awesome
discovery that cognac, caramel, saddle, chestnut, straw, khaki,
wheat, chamois, copper, oatmeal, heather, and tan all are
pretty much the same color: beige.

I have made a few purchases from the glistening-trays-full-
of-meat-pies catalog. But only for *other* people. I don't want
those glistening meat pies anywhere near my own home. And
I have also, on occasion, purchased a few theoretically provocative items of clothing from the trussed-up-women-near-a-

cozy-fireplace catalog. Recently I have been the lucky recipient of a lot of catalogs obviously aimed at yuppies-who-have-too-much-disposable-income. The particular one of which I speak bears the title "Tools for Exploration" and also makes the claim: "The World's Most Complete Selection of Unique Products for Feeling Great and Being Great." I was in kind of a slump the day it arrived. So the idea of a little help with actually *being* great sounded pretty good.

Looking back to that day, I realize that it could only have been a writing deadline that drove me to actually read the catalog in such detail. I was immediately put off by the language, which was full of annoying new-age words like "neurosonics" and "psychosensory integration." To say nothing of statements such as "the more your body-mind is stimulated with high-quality light, the better you will feel and perform," leading me to think, "okay, if we assume interrogation under a bare lightbulb is probably *low*-quality light stimulation, I wonder how much good just staring pie-eyed into my desk lamp would do me?"

Anyway, I decided to send for something. Right off the bat I found myself shying away from "a unique opportunity to hear the haunting sounds of space." Intuitively I felt that a little of "the haunting sounds of space" probably went a long way. I also did not feel drawn to the "hypno-peripheral processing" of Dr. Lloyd Glauberman . . . perhaps because of the catalog description: "He tells you two stories simultaneously—one in each ear—and the best surprise may be the change you feel taking place within you," which sounded uncannily like having dinner with my parents (and the change I recall taking place within me then didn't feel like anything I wanted to duplicate so soon again). The best deal seemed to be The Mind's Eye Mastermind ($199.95), described as "the ideal product for someone who's new to us and for whom every dollar counts." Especially after I read that the catalog people would loan me any item for a test period. That was it. No more calls. We have a winner.

While I awaited the arrival of the Mastermind, my life cooperated by disintegrating into the kind of chaos that begged for high-quality light. First, I told this friend of mine that I would try living with Tex, a hyper dog she rescued from some sort of living hell that was presumably worse than the one I generally inhabit. I was kind of thinking about getting a second dog anyway—even though I sort of already *had* a second dog because my neighbor's dog Beau would climb under my front fence or jump *over* my back fence and come in through my dog door every morning, arriving *on my bed* at about seven, which is where he would stay until I drove him home. (If I was too lazy, then he would also spend the night and of course be entitled to a continental breakfast.) (Okay, okay . . . I know.) The thing that interested me about the slightly annoying Tex was that he seemed to have an affinity for "two-guys-on-a-rope," a game which my dog Lewis would like to play twenty-four hours a day. The way the game works is that player A (Lewis) shoves a damp filthy tattered rope into the legs of player B (not me if I can help it) and then whines until player B allows herself to be pulled around the room until her arms come loose from their sockets. That Tex (who looks like a short Italian guy with a height complex wearing a French-cut T-shirt because he's really been working on his biceps) seemed immediately willing to play this game was thrilling. So I told my friend she could leave him at my house and I went off in my car to buy dog meals for two and a half. On my way home from the store I spotted a little fluffy dog cheerfully trotting down the Pacific Coast Highway—already resembling the tufted bath mat that he was destined to become if he did not select a new location for his constitutional. So I stopped and put him in my car, intending to drive him home and yell at his owners. That was *before* I realized he was wearing no tags.

Well? What was I supposed to do? Take him to the pound?

Not too many minutes after we got back to my place it hit me like a tornado of terror. I had *four fucking dogs!* But wait! What was that box sitting on my doorstep? Could it be a package containing the "powerful brain entrainment tones" of Mastermind, designed to help me not just feel great but *be* great? Boy, did I need it now!

The box contained a pair of black glasses that reminded me of the X-ray specs I used to send for from the back of comics. The main difference was that these had a row of tiny lightbulbs on the inside of the frames and were rigged so that you could hook them up to a control panel (along with the headphones of your choice) and then the plug the whole thing into the wall socket. I decided program #2 was a good place to start—"a quick romp to the theta state" (25 minutes). Although this was the first I'd even heard of the theta state, I enjoy a quick romp as much as the next person, so I lay down on the couch and tried to concentrate on the sound of an electronic *dudududududud* that accompanied what looked like turquoise, red, and orange vibrating concentric circles until the phone rang during minute 8. At that point, because my eyes were burning, I got up to find the phone and simultaneously realized that I was now being followed *way* too energetically by *four entire dogs.* Suddenly I was living in the middle of a cattle drive. There were clouds of dust and thundering hoofbeats. I swear to you there was tumbleweed. It was so unnerving that I decided to take a short break from "being great" to go out and post FOUND signs (featuring a polaroid I took of the new fluffy dog) onto every flat surface for a radius of miles around my neighborhood. I also put ads in all the local papers.

By the time I got home, I was in desperate need of some kind of mind alteration. But instead of opting for my usual cheap, tawdry solutions I hooked myself up again, this time selecting program #12, which promised "Revitalization: designed to reduce tension while imparting a renewed sense of vigor" (25 minutes). Sounded good to me! This time the audio portion was kind of like ninedeeninedeeninedeenine, although the visual portion looked quite a bit like the concentric circle vibrations from program #2. Nevertheless, *this* time I was determined to stick with it for the full 25 minutes. I *deserved* a real shot at greatness.

At minute 11 I experienced some anxiety when I heard the gardeners enter my backyard. I was briefly concerned about their reactions when they peered into my living room and saw me hooked up to sci-fi goggles. But I overcame my embarrassment and resumed my focus. When I emerged about twenty-five minutes later, I was not only being stared at by four dogs, but the room was also alive with an odor that indicated that one or more of them was not enjoying his meals as much as I had previously supposed. It occurred to me that I was neither feeling great nor being great.

But at least the dogs were all very glad to see me. So the next day I sent back the glasses. And I kept the dogs.

Extend a social invitation to someone
you've always been afraid to approach.

• • •

My Romantic Dinner
with Fabio

Monday morning the sun staggered sleepily through the
grimy blinds of my vine-covered Malibu bungalow as I awakened to the sounds of a ringing telephone. Lazily I stretched
out my long tanned limbs like a tawny lynx as I struggled to
answer it, reaching over the four sleeping dogs between me
and the nightstand. It was a woman from *TV Guide*. "We
would like you to write an article entitled 'My Romantic Dinner with Fabio,' " she said. My tender lips trembled as I silently mouthed the words. "My Romantic Dinner with Fabio??"
I shook my tousled mane of raven hair as I tried to compre-
hend the idea of me and Fabio ever, even momentarily, sharing the same breathing space on the planet. Until now, it
seemed just a shade less likely than a surprise announcement
that I had been appointed the new replacement for Les Aspin.

"Yes, okay. I'll do it," I heard myself whisper. "His people will call you," she replied. "They would like to do it on Wednesday."

Within hours I was on the phone with Peter Paul, Fabio's manager. He was anxious to tell me about "Fabio's message of support for the rights and needs of women." Plus his new video, his newly renovated international 900 number, his perfume endorsement, and his future plans to make action-adventure movies with video game merchandising and Marvel comics tie-ins. My pale hands began to tremble as I realized that for the first time in my life my bosom was starting to heave.

TUESDAY

I arise bright and early and head off to the store to purchase *Pirate,* the romance novel that Fabio sort of wrote. As I inspect the only cover photo I have ever seen of an author scowling, bare-chested, and wielding a scabbard (except, of course, for the one of Joyce Carol Oates) I cannot help feeling a pang of envy at the way my companion-to-be has achieved a career as a best-selling author without having to suffer the fatigue, torture, and endless irritations of actually having to sit down and write. If only he will share his secrets with me.

By the time I get home, his press kit has arrived and soon I am awash in articles about Fabio published in every imaginable publication, as well, of course, as thousands of vivid color photographs. Fabio, astride a motorcycle, bare-chested and scowling. Fabio holding a bouquet of roses, dressed only in tuxedo pants and suspenders, scowling as he heads out the door to the world's most casual black-tie event. The anticipation is building. Yes, yes, I think to myself, I have dined before with many scowling guys. But always in the past were they wearing two or more shirts.

WEDNESDAY

I spend the day consumed with but a single thought: What exactly is the appropriate attire to wear to a romantic dinner with Fabio? I try on millions of outfits, unsure of what I am even after. Perhaps it's the name that's so intimidating. Maybe if I think of him as "Ricky." Then I only have to answer the question, "What do I wear out to dinner with Ricky?" Much much more doable.

I have been told a limousine will pick me up at 6:45. By then my bosom is heaving so hard, I tuck some smelling salts in my purse. Eagerly I watch as the clock turns to 6:45, then 7:00, then 7:10. By 7:15 I am beginning to accumulate a light sprinkling of dog hairs. One dog has placed a filthy sock full of tennis balls on my lap, another has started a small snag in my pantyhose. Undaunted, I continue to wait breathlessly. But alas . . . by 7:30 I grow concerned. Mayhap he has been waylaid by danger? I daren't phone his people for fear he will chortle scornfully and call me "a demanding little minx" like he did the girl in his book. So instead, I relax, take off my jacket, and fix myself half a toasted bagel.

By 7:45 I am beginning to doze when I am awakened by the plaintive howls of my dogs. Hastily I re-dress and run to peer out my front window. The gate opens and . . . a limousine driver just stands there, holding my front gate open. When he keeps on just standing there, I grab my purse and head out the door. And behold! Out in my driveway: a limousine full of Fabio. When I realize this is part of the ancient Buccaneer custom of "waiting for the woman out in the car but also bringing *two* beautiful bouquets of yellow roses to distract her so she won't be pissed," I am appeased. Plus, there is another special surprise just for me. Fabio is wearing a shirt! A red cotton pullover with a V-neck zipper, under a blue-gray sportcoat. I am deeply, deeply relieved. We say hello. Our eyes meet and . . . yep. My new friend Ricky looks just exactly like Fabio.

The limo whisks us off to Geoffrey's, one of the prettiest restaurants on the Malibu coast. Although I have been there many many times before, this is the only visit at which the entire female staff turned out to give us a tour. We are seated at a lovely veranda table with a view of the whole coast at night. The nearby heat lamp casts a golden glow on our powerful bodies. I ask him to tell me about his dogs, one of the things I know we have in common. His face lights up as he speaks fondly of his three purebred 175-pound Great Danes, one of which is on a list of "The 22 Most Beautiful Animals in the World." I have never seen this list, so I do not know if any of my dogs made it. Nevertheless, we begin to bond on the topic of dog-related damage. *"Oh yeah, nose prints,"* he tells me. *"The house have a lot of door windows and they have the nose prints all over. The house where I was staying, they almost chew through a wall,"* he confides. *"I am screaming at them when I catch them and they look at me like 'I didn't do anything.' Except they are covered with white stuff on their big black noses from where they eat the wall."* He laughs bravely through his tears. *"It's a beautiful thing because they give unconditional love. Very hard to find."*

The waiter arrives and Fabio orders oysters on the half

shell. I order a Caesar salad. *"You're not a vegetarian, are you?"* he asks. *"I don't want you to turn into a cucumber."* Our eyes meet again as I take out a pile of his publicity photos. "This guy lying facedown in the pounding surf, barechested and scowling," I say to him, "what is he thinking to himself when he poses like this?"

"He is saying 'I am ready to seduce you. Let me be your man. Let me make you feel like a real woman,' " he tells me.

"How about, 'Let me come into your life and get dampness all over your couch?' " I suggest.

He grins at me as he eats an oyster. *"You are funny girl,"* he says. *"Bon appetite."*

As we dine on pasta with shiitake mushrooms (or "shtucky mushrooms" as Fabio calls them) we speak of many things. HIS HOPES: *"I want to create a new superhero that appeals to men AND women. Schwarzenegger appeals only to men."* HIS DREAMS: *"When you branch yourself out as a business person you see many opportunities."* "So will we one day awaken to see 'Fabio's House of Pancakes?' " I ask. *"I like food,"* he replies. *"I would do healthy stuff. Shakes and omelettes."* THE DIFFICULTIES MEN AND WOMEN HAVE COMMUNICATING: *"People don't say anything honest to each other,"* he says wistfully. *"People like to play games. I don't like to play games. I don't want to play games. I hate to play games."* "What *kind* of games exactly?" I ask as I quietly push the Parcheesi board to the back of my purse where it will not upset him. *"Mind games,"* he replies, *"like when you see that a person really likes you and she plays very hard to get. I don't like that,"* he says, as he graciously accepts the rest of my dinner.

My bosom is heaving, my trachea engorged with partially

swallowed pasta, as I decide it is time to find out just who *is* this MAN THEY CALL FABIO?

"Tell me," I say as he gazes into my upturned face, "what would you do if you kissed a woman and she slobbered on you?"

"Nothing turns me off about a woman," he replies.

"What would happen if you looked over at me and I had just dropped a huge forkful of pasta onto my lap?" I rally.

"I would eat it," he laughs. I hope he likes pasta with dog hair, I think to myself.

"What if you were making out and a woman's stomach started to rumble?" I continue.

"I will try and get her a Pepto Bismol," he says.

"And what if you went to her house and were making love and you found there were crumbs in her bed?"

"No big deal," he answers. *"I block out. I don't pay attention."*

Things are moving very fast. There is still one question unanswered. "What if she got drunk and threw up on you?" I ask breathlessly, the wind in my hair.

"Well, that's heavy," he admits. *"I guess I go to the bathroom and try to clean up as best I can.*

"Let me esplain you something," he says, as the gentle breeze blows softly through the remaining pasta. *"Life is very easy. People complicates their life."*

"I think life is kind of difficult," I confess.

"YOU make your life difficult," he tells me. *"Probably you didn't let anybody at your same level come into your life. When somebody is equal, nobody has control. When you want to have control, the person you let come into your life is*

not gonna be your equal. The best feeling in love is to surrender to the other person."

Then he drops the bombshell that will change our future forever. *"Now I have a person I spend time with. I'm really crazy about this person,"* he says. *"She's a model-actress, extremely attractive, has a super super personality."*

Yes, but what does he *see* in her? my heart cries out in the night. "How long has this been going on?" I ask quietly.

"A month," he tells me. *"We have a great time and we are friends. We really don't want to rush. People always rush to make love."*

"So the relationship hasn't been consummated yet?" I ask, thinking this may be more information than I need.

"We have time," he tells me. *"Women sometime they rush and for the man it doesn't mean anything. What me and this person did is we know each other well first."*

I sigh deeply as I gaze mournfully through the pain, past the piece of lettuce that is resting on my knee, off into the depths of the deep blue sea. And I recall the words he spoke to me back then: *"The dogs no inside the house."* I thought I could change him but I knew then that we could never be.

And so we went our separate ways—he back to his life of endless publicity tours and millions of business opportunities, and I back to my house full of dog-hair wads the size of a man's toupee. But late at night, whenever the gentle breeze blows through the pasta, I will remember the greatest love that never was. I will remember.